Making Use of Ruby

Making Use of RUBY

Suresh Mahadevan

Wiley Publishing, Inc.

Publisher: Robert Ipsen
Editor: Ben Ryan
Developmental Editor: Kathryn A. Malm
Managing Editor: Pamela Hanley
New Media Editor: Brian Snapp
Text Design & Composition: Wiley Composition Services

Designations used by companies to distinguish their products are often claimed as trademarks. In all instances where Wiley Publishing, Inc., is aware of a claim, the product names appear in initial capital or ALL CAPITAL LETTERS. Readers, however, should contact the appropriate companies for more complete information regarding trademarks and registration.

This book is printed on acid-free paper. ∞

For general information on our other products and services please contact our Customer Care Department within the United States at (800) 762-2974, outside the United States at (317) 572-3993 or fax (317) 572-4002.

Wiley also publishes its books in a variety of electronic formats. Some content that appears in print may not be available in electronic books.

Library of Congress Cataloging-in-Publication Data:

ISBN # 0-471-21972-X

Printed in the United States of America

10 9 8 7 6 5 4 3 2 1

Contents

Introduction

In this information age, portability is one of the important features that everybody looks forward to in a programming language. Language being portable means that it should be able to run on any operating system. Moreover, it should be able to provide a similar performance on all the operating systems. Users will find Ruby extremely useful in terms of portability. Ruby can be run on most versions of UNIX, DOS, Windows 95/98/NT, Mac, and OS/2.

Ruby is a portable, interpreted, object-oriented programming language. It combines remarkable power with very clear syntax. Moreover, its high-level built-in data structures, combined with dynamic typing and dynamic binding, make it very attractive for scripting.

Do you want to know whether Ruby is popular? Based on recent reports, Ruby is more popular than Python, another scripting language, in Japan. Check this URL—www.ruby-lang.org/en/magazine.html—to find various articles in different information technology (IT) magazines.

Our job is to solve problems, not spoonfeed compilers, so we like dynamic languages that adapt to us, without arbitrary, rigid rules. We need clarity so we can communicate using our code. We value conciseness and the ability to express a requirement in code accurately and efficiently. The less code we write, the less that can go wrong. (And our wrists and fingers are thankful, too.)

We want to be as productive as possible, so we want our code to run the first time; time spent in the debugger is time stolen from the development clock. It also helps if we can try out code as we edit it; if you have to wait for a 2-hour make cycle, you may as well be using punch cards and submitting your work for batch compilation.

When we discovered Ruby, we realized that we'd found what we'd been looking for. More than any other language with which we have worked, Ruby stays out of your way. You can concentrate on solving the problem at hand, instead of struggling with compiler and language issues. That's how it can help you become a better programmer: by giving you the chance to spend your time creating solutions for your users, not for the compiler.

Dave Thomas and Andy Hunt,
The Pragmatic Programmer's Guide

Most of all, Ruby puts the fun back into programming. When was the last time you had fun writing a program—a program that worked the first time; a program that you could read next week, next month, or next year and still understand exactly what it does? We find Ruby to be a breath of fresh air in the dense, often hectic world of programming. In fact, we see nothing but smiles after we present Ruby to programmers.

www.rubycentral.com

This book is an attempt to bridge the ever-increasing gap between the market demand and the availability of Ruby expertise. The first step to becoming an expert is to get an in-depth knowledge of Ruby, and this is exactly what this book has to offer. It begins with the basics of scripting and moves seamlessly over to the programming intricacies.

Along with conceptual information, this book also will provide extensive practical exercises to allow readers to gain valuable real-life exposure in creating different types of applications.

The aim of this book is to make learning an enjoyable and energizing process.

Overview of Ruby

Ruby has features that are similar to those of Smalltalk, Perl, and Python. Perl, Python, and Smalltalk are scripting languages. Smalltalk is a true object-oriented language. Ruby, like Smalltalk, is a perfect object-oriented language. Using Ruby syntax is much easier than using Smalltalk syntax.

Therefore, Smalltalk users will find learning and playing around with Ruby quite easy. A special feature of Ruby is that it has the useful features of Perl, Python, and Smalltalk. For instance, Ruby comes in with regular expressions, which is one of the major features of Perl and Python. In addition, you can easily access the operating-system features in both Perl and Python.

History of Ruby

Yukihiro Matsumoto of Japan is the founder of Ruby. Ruby was created in 1993. However, it was only after 1995 that it became popular. The updated news for Ruby lovers is that Ruby has become more popular than Python in Japan. Until recently, Ruby's adoption outside Japan was hampered by the lack of documentation in English. There are not many books available on Ruby. This makes it extremely difficult for Ruby to penetrate the other parts of the world. However, the year 2002 may just be the beginning of the rise in the popularity of Ruby because a lot of books in English will be released in 2002.

NOTE You can find the name Yukihiro Matsumoto on the Ruby mailing list at www.ruby-lang.org. Matsumoto is also known as Matz in the Ruby community.

Before, we move on to discuss the features of Ruby, we will conclude this section with what Matz has to say about the evolution of Ruby:

Well, Ruby was born on February 24, 1993. I was talking with my colleague about the possibility of an object-oriented scripting language. I knew Perl (Perl4, not Perl5), but I didn't like it really, because it had the smell of a toy language (it still has). The object-oriented language seemed very promising.

I knew Python then. But I didn't like it, because I didn't think it was a true object-oriented language—OO features appeared to be add-on to the language. As a language maniac and OO fan for 15 years, I really wanted a genuine object-oriented, easy-to-use scripting language. I looked for but couldn't find one.

So I decided to make it. It took several months to make the interpreter run. I put it the features I love to have in my language, such as iterators, exception handling, and garbage collection.

Then I reorganized the features of Perl into a class library and implement them. I posted Ruby 0.95 to the Japanese domestic newsgroups in December 1995.

Features of Ruby

Ruby is an open-source, general-purpose, interpreted, and powerful server-side scripting language. Ruby also is freely available on the Web, but it is subject to a license. You can obtain the license from the URL www.ruby-lang.org/en/license.txt. With Ruby, programming becomes very easy. One of the major advantages is that Ruby provides a simple interpreter, unlike other programming languages. Using other programming language compilers, a programmer spends maximum effort in trying to get over the complexities of the compiler instead of concentrating on the actual coding part. This becomes frustrating at times for the programmer. With Ruby, you need not worry about all these issues; you can concentrate specifically on coding. The another advantage is Ruby is an untyped language. With untyped languages, you need not bother to define everything before you start executing the code. However, one thing you need to remember is that Ruby is an interpreted language. Interpreted languages are slower when compared to compiled languages. Let us discuss some of the salient features of Ruby.

Easy

Ruby has a clean and easy syntax that allows a new developer to learn Ruby very quickly and easily. It will require a lesser effort for people who have some programming knowledge. The syntax of Ruby is similar to that of many programming languages such as C++ and Perl. Therefore, it becomes very easy for programmers to learn Ruby and start writing programs. Ruby is a perfect object-oriented language, unlike some languages, such as Python, which only supports the concept of object orientation. In fact, Ruby is a simplification of these languages, and it does not require any extra effort to learn an unfamiliar concept, syntax, or keyword.

With Ruby, you will be surprised at the amount of code you can churn out in a day. The reason is that after you learn the basic syntax, which is easy compared with other languages, you will not have many errors in your code. In addition, the Ruby interpreter is fantastic. There are no major hassles in using it. Because of all these factors, the time you spend in debugging code is minimal. Fortunately, in Ruby you do not have to go through the pain of putting semicolons at the end of each and every statement. All these features make Ruby a very good and simple language to work with.

Scalable

UNIX shell scripting languages are fairly easy and can handle simple tasks very easily and efficiently. However, when you add more features to a script, the script becomes very large, complicated, and slow. You are unable to reuse your code, and even small projects require huge scripts. Ruby provides a better structure for large programs. You can write modules in Ruby and then reuse those modules across different code. Ruby also provides many built-in modules to help you in system management tasks, networking, socket programming, and graphic user interface (GUI) programming.

Object-Oriented

As stated earlier, Ruby is a true object-oriented programming language. All the features of Ruby are implemented as objects. Ruby shows all the characteristics of an object-oriented language. Ruby shows multiple inheritance indirectly like Java. Java implements multiple inheritance by using interfaces, whereas Ruby implements the same by using mixins.

Extensible

There are many libraries that provide functionality that may be useful to have in your programs. It does not make sense to rewrite all these libraries in Ruby. In addition, there are occasions when you may need performance that is better than the performance of an interpreted language such as Ruby. It will be useful, therefore, if you could write the time-critical code in an efficient language and simply call it from your Ruby code. Ruby helps you to take care of both these situations. Using Ruby, you can easily write extensions in C/C++ that hook seamlessly into Ruby's environment. It would seem that they are simply other pieces of Ruby code. You can create Ruby extensions in C/C++ using dynamic or static binding.

You can even go the other way around and embed a complete Ruby interpreter into a C program, allowing you to use its scripting facilities rather than having to write your own purpose-built engine. The fact is that with Ruby extensions the sky is the limit!

Rich Core Library

Many development modules are built into Ruby. A programmer can make use of these modules directly. In addition to modules that work on all platforms, the library has modules that are specific to a particular platform or environment.

Ruby built-in modules perform all types of usual tasks, such as HTTP, FTP, POP, SMTP, and many other services. Using the rich core library, you can write applications for downloading a Web page, connecting to a database, developing a GUI, and so on.

Web Scripting Support and Data Handling

Ruby can be used for developing Internet and intranet applications. You can even write a Web server using Ruby. You can write Common Gateway Interface (CGI) scripts using Ruby. You can even embed Ruby programs into Hypertext Markup Language (HTML). You also can write high-end Extensible Markup Language (XML) applications using Ruby.

Object Distribution

Using distributed Ruby, you can create a server object and expose that object. Next, you can write a client program and access the server object. This becomes similar to Java's Remote Method Invocation (RMI). All this can be done very easily in Ruby.

Databases

You can use the built-in objects from the various libraries that are available to make Ruby talk to a database. Using Ruby, you can easily connect to DB2, MySQL, Oracle, and Sybase. ODBC drivers are being written to connect Ruby to popular databases.

GUI Programming

There are several GUIs, such as Tcl/Tk, GTK, and OpenGL. You can download the extensions for these GUIs from the Ruby Application Archive (RAA). The Ruby Application Archive is a Web page that acts as a repository for many Ruby applications.

Exception Handling

You execute a program, and suddenly, an unknown error pops up. The program will end abruptly without knowing what to do and exit. Exceptional cases such as these are termed *exceptions*. To handle such exceptions, you need to add exception-handling code in your main code. With Ruby, exception handling becomes clean and simple. Using exception handling in Ruby, the programmer needs to make less effort to debug an error.

Portable

Ruby can be installed in Windows and POSIX environments. Code written under Windows can be run under Linux and vice versa unless you are not trying to access features specific to that operating system. Therefore, when you say a code is portable, it means lesser expenditure and wider distribution.

Freeware

Ruby is a freeware and can be redistributed freely in the source form subject to the license we discussed earlier. Programmers and users are allowed to use Ruby's source code in any desired way. You can download the Ruby source code, modify the code, and even distribute the code. Ruby is also free for commercial use. You can make applications in Ruby and upload it to the RAA for other users to access. In the same way, you can download many of the applications created by different users from this archive page.

Ruby versus Other Languages

Languages can be divided into two types, compiled languages and scripting languages. Applications created using compiled languages are faster than those created using scripting languages. With compiled languages, you can easily access the operating system features, whereas with scripting languages you cannot. However, nowadays the distinction between compiled and scripting languages is not the same. Scripting languages are as fast as compiled languages. In addition, you can access the operating system features by using scripting languages such as Perl, Python, and Ruby.

Ruby can be compared with other programming languages easily because of its resemblance to many programming languages, such as C,

Perl, Python, Java, Smalltalk, and the shell scripts of UNIX. You actually can find a lot of syntax common between Ruby and C. Ruby can be compared with Perl and Python because both Perl and Python are scripting languages. What you can do in Ruby you also can do in Perl and Python. The only difference is that Ruby is much more flexible than Perl and Python. Creating applications in Ruby is much easier than creating applications in Perl and Python. Ruby can be compared with Smalltalk because both are true object-oriented programming languages. Ruby is similar to Java only in terms of showing multiple inheritance. Both Ruby and Java implement multiple inheritance indirectly, unlike C++, which shows multiple inheritance directly.

How This Book Is Organized

This book shrugs away from the traditional content-based approach and uses the problem-based approach to deliver the concepts of Ruby. Problems used in the book are presented against the backdrop of real-life scenarios. Each problem is followed by a task list that helps you to solve the given problem, in the process delivering the concepts and their implementation. This practical approach will help you to understand the real-life application of the language and its use in various scenarios. Moreover, to provide appropriate learning experience, the concepts will be supported adequately by case studies that will be formulated in such a way that they provide you with a frame of reference.

This book is organized into two parts. The first part involves programming with Ruby using arrays, hashes, methods, and modules. And the second part delves into developing advanced applications with Ruby using CGI, GUI, and networking features.

Chapter 1 introduces you to Ruby. It also guides you to where you can obtain Ruby and its documentation. Finally, it instructs you on how to install Ruby and discusses the different modes in which you can run Ruby.

Chapter 2 deals purely with object orientation. This chapter gives you an overview of object-orientation concepts. You also learn to implement object orientation by using Ruby.

Chapter 3 introduces you to the different data types in Ruby. It discusses how to implement arrays and hashes in Ruby. You will move a step further and learn how to implement ranges in Ruby.

Chapter 4 introduces you to the various control structures supported by Ruby. Then you will learn to implement blocks and iterators in Ruby. Finally, you will learn the important concept of regular expressions.

Chapter 5 discusses different kinds of methods. You will learn to pass an array to a method. Then the chapter will introduce you to modules. Finally, you will implement mixins by using modules.

Chapter 6 deals with the various input and output statements. It also deals with the various methods related to the file and input-output (I/O) classes.

Chapter 7 deals with exceptions. You will learn to handle exceptions. You also will learn about the exception class. Then you will learn how to raise exceptions. Finally, you will learn about the catch and throw methods.

Chapter 8 discusses a most interesting concept—multithreading. You will learn to create and manipulate threads. You will learn about the mutex class. You will learn how to schedule threads. Finally, you will get to know about multiprocessing.

Chapter 9 goes to the Web. It discusses CGI programming. You will learn how to write CGI scripts by using the CGI class. Then you also will learn about cookies and sessions. Finally, you will learn about eRuby.

Chapter 10 moves one step ahead and discusses GUI programming using Tk. You will learn about the various widgets you can use in a GUI application.

Chapter 11 discusses running Ruby on Windows. It discusses the Win32API class. Finally, you will learn to use automation features in Ruby.

Chapter 12 delves into network programming in Ruby using sockets. It discusses the TCPServer and TCPSocket classes. Then it discusses distributed Ruby. Finally, you will learn how to implement HTTP, FTP, SMTP, and POP3 protocols using Ruby.

Finally, Appendix A gives a brief introduction to Ruby Extensions with C, and **Appendix B** discusses the concept of tainting.

Who Should Read This Book

This book will be a guide for readers with basic knowledge of programming. For those with intermediary knowledge of Ruby, the book covers the advanced concepts of Ruby too. This book will be of great help to people with the following job titles:

- Software engineers
- Web application developers
- Information application developers

This book will provide the necessary skills to create GUI, networking, and Web applications. It also will talk about extending and embedding Ruby applications.

Tools You Will Need

For performing the tasks in this book, you will need a Pentium 200-MHz computer with a minimum of 64 MB of RAM (128 MB of RAM recommended). You also will need the following software:

- Linux 7.1 or Windows 95/98/2000/NT operating system
- Apache 1.3.19-5 Web server
- Internet Explorer 5.0 or above Web browser
- Ruby 1.6.6

What's on the Web Site

The following will be available on the site www.wiley.com/compbooks/ Makinguse:

- Ruby 1.6.6
- All the code snippets used in this book

Scenario

All problem statements in this book are based on the scenario of Knowledge, Inc. The following section delineates the setup of Knowledge, Inc., and its future plans.

Knowledge, Inc.

Knowledge, Inc., was set up by Mark Bates, who wanted to set up a library equipped with all kinds of books and use his library to spread knowledge. In 1973, Mark established a small library in California and soon extended the services that his library offered to cover various states, such as Georgia and Texas. Today, Knowledge, Inc., is a major bookshop with various outlets across the United States.

The transformation of the library into a bookstore took place in 1980. One fine day in the autumn of 1980, Harry, Mark's friend and business partner, came up with the idea of opening a bookshop. Mark appreciated the idea, and in 1981, Knowledge, Inc., opened its first bookshop outlet in California. Knowledge, Inc., grew at a rate of 150 percent annually, and today it is one of the largest bookstores in the United States.

The services that Knowledge, Inc., offers extend over all the major states and cities of the United States. Knowledge, Inc., has 26 outlets across the country. These outlets also perform selling operations. At present, the outlets not only sell books and other knowledge-based materials directly but also receive orders for books over the telephone. Knowledge, Inc., fills orders received on the telephone through various courier services.

Knowledge, Inc., found general acceptance through its dedicated and personalized customer service. The financial presentation in the last general body meeting indicates that the profits of Knowledge, Inc., have increased manifold. The board members have decided to increase profits further by going online on the Web.

In the last board meeting, the following developments took place:

- Most of the competitors of Knowledge, Inc., either own Web sites or are in the process of launching e-commerce services.
- Recent customer feedback shows that most professionals want to buy online.
- The existing customers are in favor of online library transactions.
- Overhead is increasing because Knowledge, Inc., has to employ many people to manage the growing business.

After extensive research into current trends in the book market, Peter Garner, the head of the Marketing Department, proposed the following approaches to tackle the current problems:

- With the rise of the Internet, online selling has become very productive.
- Most people are in favor of online buying because it saves time and is easy to access.
- The Internet is an effective medium to reach new customers. It also will hasten use of the traditional approach to acquiring new customers.
- Online selling will help to save resources because the automation of services will reduce team size.

In the next couple of years, Knowledge, Inc., is targeting the creation of a customer base all around the world. At present, it plans to target customers through its online Web site. Using the Web site, it also can increase the number of its customers within the United States.

At the end of the board meeting, the proposal to set up an online site for Knowledge, Inc., was supported unanimously. The Electronic Data Processing (EDP) Department will handle the task of creating the online site. Paul Anderson has been nominated as the project manager. He is the head of a team of competent designers and programmers. A quality assurance team and a graphics team also have been assigned to support the development team. The management wants the online bookstore to be developed in an upcoming scripting language, Ruby.

In the next few months, the team will endeavor to ensure zero-defect software development that is in line with client requirements. After the online site for Knowledge, Inc., has been set up, customers will be able to log onto the Web site www.knowledgethruweb.com and carry out transactions without any difficulty.

CHAPTER

1

An Introduction to Ruby

OBJECTIVES

In this chapter, you will learn to:

- ✔ Identify the scenarios where Ruby can be used
- ✔ Obtain Ruby and its documentation
- ✔ Examine system requirements of Ruby
- ✔ Install Ruby
- ✔ Identify the different modes of running Ruby

Getting Started

This chapter gives you an insight into Ruby. This chapter will also discuss the system requirements for Ruby. In addition, you will learn about the Web sites where you can obtain Ruby documentation. We also will discuss the Web sites from which you can download various Ruby applications.

About Ruby

Problem Statement

Knowledge, Inc., plans to go online with a Web site that allows it to sell its books through the Web. The development team of Knowledge, Inc., has programmers who have about five to six years' experience in Perl. However, the development team of Knowledge, Inc., is not very keen on developing the Web site in Perl. One of the main reasons for this is that members of the team want to use a new language. Another reason for this is that even after having used Perl for so many years, members of the team believe that Perl has a cumbersome syntax. They want to learn a language that is relatively new and simple. Top management has agreed to develop the Web site in a language that is similar to but better than Perl. However, management wants the project to be completed in a very short time.

After having long discussions with various experts, management has decided to develop the Web site in a new and upcoming language known as Ruby. Top management has hired Mike, who has about nine years' experience in programming. He has worked in Ruby for nearly three years. Management has selected Mike to be the technical lead in this project.

Mike has been given the task of understanding the requirements of the project, obtaining Ruby for the development team, and getting Ruby running.

Task List

- ✔ **Determine the requirements of the project.**
- ✔ **Obtain Ruby and its documentation.**
- ✔ **Determine the system requirements of Ruby.**
- ✔ **Install Ruby.**
- ✔ **Discuss the different modes of running Ruby.**

Determine the Requirements of the Project

Before deciding on the software application and hardware platforms to use for this project, let us understand the requirements of the project (Table 1.1).

Table 1.1   Requirements of Knowledge, Inc.

Development time	The entire application needs to be developed in three months.
Speed	Knowledge, Inc., wants a computerized system that enables customers to buy books easily and quickly.
Accessibility	Knowledge, Inc., wants a system that enables customers to buy books online from any part of the world.
Unique features	Because Knowledge, Inc., also has its own library for its customers, management wants a system that automatically notifies customers of the return date of the books through email messages.
Other features	Management wants the application to be powerful, robust, and scalable.

Obtain Ruby and Its Documentation

As we learned from Matz, Ruby 0.95 was posted to Japanese domestic groups in December 1995. Afterwards, various versions of Ruby were released. At present, the latest stable version is Ruby 1.6.7. Like other open-source-code projects, Ruby also follows the same version-numbering system. In this system, the even version numbers are stable, whereas the odd version numbers are unstable. For example, versions 1.0, 1.2, 1.4, and 1.6 are stable, and versions 1.1, 1.3, and 1.5 are unstable.

You can download Ruby from one of these two sites:

- www.ruby-lang.org
- www.rubycentral.com

You can get all the relevant information about Ruby on these two sites. You can get the online book about Ruby, *Pragmatic Programmers Guide for Ruby*, by Dave Thomas and Andrew Hunt, as a downloadable in the form of an HTML or PDF document on the site www.ruby-lang.org. All the documentation for Ruby has existed only in the Japanese language. The *Pragmatic Programmers Guide for Ruby* is the first English documentation for Ruby. You can get frequently asked questions (FAQs) regarding Ruby from the site www.rubycentral.com. You also can get software downloads for Linux and Windows at these sites. You can get the various slides of the different presentations made for Ruby across the world. You also have the Ruby Application Archive (RAA) Web page. This Web page can be found at www.ruby-lang.org/en/raa.html. The RAA consists of Ruby applications posted by various Ruby followers. Finally, you have the mailing list that consists of members of the Ruby community. You can join this mailing list and exchange mail with members of this community.

Determine the System Requirements of Ruby

Ruby can run on Windows and all versions of UNIX. Even the Macintosh operating system supports Ruby. The hardware requirements for installing Ruby are the same as the hardware requirements for the underlying operating system on which you have chosen to run Ruby. Therefore, you do not require any special hardware for installing Ruby.

Install Ruby

In this section we will look at installing Ruby on both Windows and UNIX.

Installing Ruby on Windows

You download Ruby installation files for Windows from either the Ruby-Central site or the Wiley site. The URLs for both are:

- http://dev.rubycentral.com/downloads/ruby-install.html
- www.wiley.com/compbooks/makinguse

From these sites, download the RubyXXX-X.exe files, where XXX-X is the latest version number, to your local computer. When you double-click the file, the Ruby installation wizard starts. Follow the different steps in the wizard and you will get Ruby installed for Windows. Here are the detailed steps for installing Ruby on Windows:

1. Double-click the **RubyXXX-X.exe** file. The Ruby installation wizard starts (Figure 1.1).
2. Click Next to move to the Important Information page of the wizard (Figure 1.2). This page displays the contents of the **Readme.txt** file.

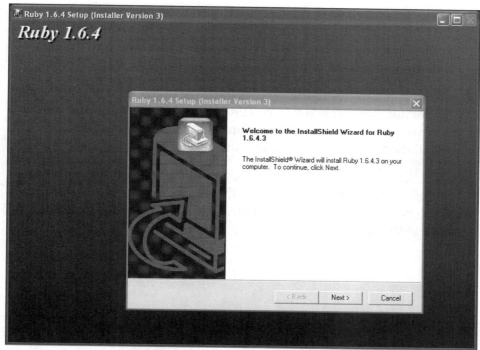

Figure 1.1   Ruby installation wizard.

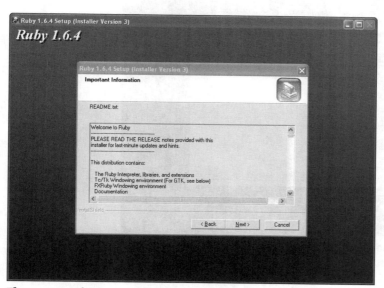

Figure 1.2   The Important Information page of the installation wizard.

3. Click Next to move to the Choose Destination Location of the wizard (Figure 1.3). By default, on the Windows platform Ruby installs in the **C:\Ruby** folder. You can change the destination folder by clicking the Browse button and choosing the destination folder.

4. Click Next to move to the Setup Type page of the wizard (Figure 1.4). By default, Typical is selected. The Typical setup installs the most common components of Ruby. You can choose compact or custom installation type, depending on your requirements.

5. Click Next to move to the Start Copying Files page of the wizard (Figure 1.5). Before copying files, the wizard summarizes the options you have selected. You can change the selected options by going back to the appropriate page.

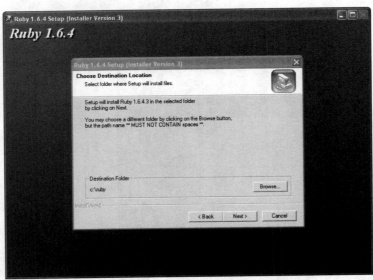

Figure 1.3 The Choose Destination Location page of the installation wizard.

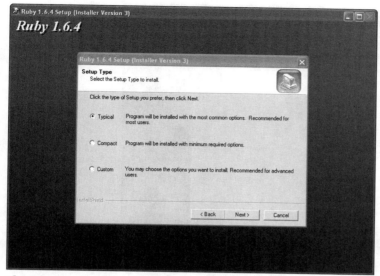

Figure 1.4 The Setup Type page of the installation wizard.

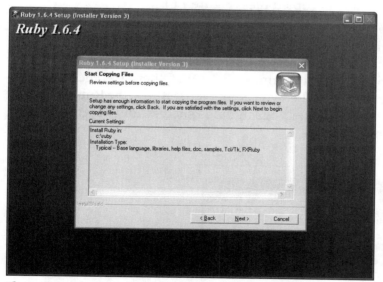

Figure 1.5 The Start Copying Files page of the installation wizard.

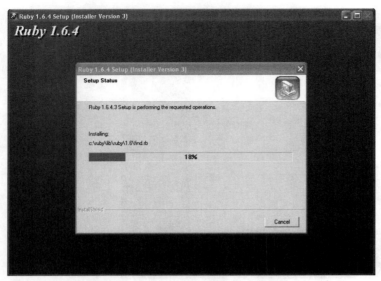

Figure 1.6   The Setup Status page of the installation wizard.

6. Click Next to start copying the Ruby files. The Setup Status page displays the status of copied files (Figure 1.6).

7. When setup finishes copying files to the destination folder, the Edit Environment? page appears (Figure 1.7). This page displays the values of Ruby environment variables, such as PATH and RUBY_TCL_DLL. If you accept the default settings, click OK. Otherwise, click Cancel and edit the settings. When you accept the settings, the Ruby Installer displays the message "Settings updated successfully." Figure 1.8 shows this message.

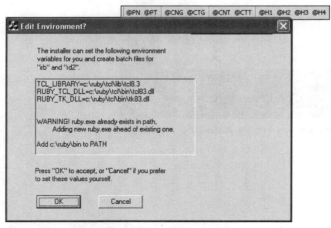

Figure 1.7   The Edit Environment? page.

Figure 1.8   The Ruby Installer message.

8. When you click OK on the Ruby Installer message box, the installation wizard displays the InstallShield Wizard Complete page, stating that the setup has finished successfully (Figure 1.9).

9. Click Finish. The setup will ask you to reboot the computer.

Installing Ruby on UNIX

If you have UNIX on your computer, you need to download the UNIX version of Ruby. The files for the UNIX version are in a compressed format. After you download your version of Ruby, you will need to unpack the downloaded files. For UNIX, the GNA gzip program performs the required action. The GNA gzip program is available at www.gnu.org/software/gzip/gzip.html.

NOTE The installation procedure for Linux is the same as UNIX installation.

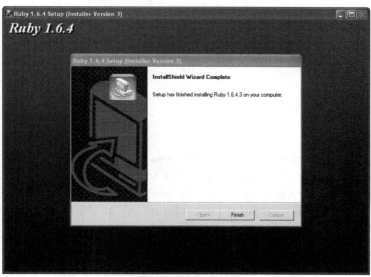

Figure 1.9   The InstallShield Wizard Complete page of the installation wizard.

Table 1.2 Software Specifications for Using Ruby with Windows

SOFTWARE	SPECIFICATION
Operating System	Windows 98
Web server	Apache 1.3.22
Web browser	Internet Explorer 5.5
Ruby	Version 1.6.5

You can choose among a number of software platforms for running Ruby. For the development of this book, the following software configuration is used (see Table 1.2).

NOTE In this book, the multithreading code is executed in Red Hat Linux 7.1.

Different Modes of Running Ruby

You can run Ruby in two modes: the interactive mode and the normal program mode.

Interactive Ruby

You can start interactive Ruby by typing `ruby` at the command prompt. The advantage of using interactive Ruby is it allows you to see results there and then. Let us learn to use interactive Ruby:

```
C:\WINDOWS>ruby
puts "Good Morning"
^D (ctrl + D)
```

The output is:

```
Good Morning
```

You type `ruby` at the command prompt and press the Enter key. The cursor comes to the next line and waits for the user to type. Just type `puts "Good Morning"` and type the end-of-file character. (In this computer, it is Control + D.) You get the output of the statement at the command prompt (Figure 1.10).

```
C:\WINDOWS>ruby
puts "Good Morning"
Good Morning
```

Figure 1.10 Interactive Ruby.

Normal Program Mode

You execute Ruby programs from the command prompt. You type `ruby` followed by the file name. For example:

```
ruby test.rb
```

where `test.rb` is the filename containing the Ruby code.

In UNIX systems you need to take care that the first line of every script should be a special comment line, something like `#!/usr/local/bin/ruby`. This comment line tells UNIX that the program `ruby` should run the particular script.

Summary

In this chapter you learned that:

- The founder of Ruby is Yukihiro Matsumoto, also known as Matz to the Ruby community.
- You can find all the latest information about Ruby on these two Web sites:
  - http://www.ruby-lang.org
  - http://www.rubycentral.com
- Ruby runs on a variety of platforms, such as Windows, Mac OS, and the various versions of UNIX.
- Ruby can be started in two different modes:
  - Interactive mode
  - Normal program mode

Ruby — A Pure Object-Oriented Language

OBJECTIVES:

In this chapter, you will learn to:

✔ Understand the meaning of object orientation

✔ Learn to implement object orientation by using Ruby

Getting Started

Since the early days of programming, programmers have devised ways and means to reduce the complexity of programs. In the beginning, machine instructions were directly fed into the computer with the help of switches. However, it was tedious to remember the instructions. Moreover, these instructions were machine-dependent. This implied that programmers needed to remember the corresponding instructions for different machines. Then came assembly-level programming, which used mnemonic codes for machine instructions. With the introduction of assembly-level language, programming became much simpler. In assembly-level language, a translator called an assembler was used to convert these mnemonic codes into machine instructions. However, the problem was that even these mnemonic codes were not completely machine-independent. Therefore, there was always a search for a complete machine-independent language.

Then followed the development of higher-level languages, such as BASIC, Pascal, and FORTRAN. With the introduction of these higher-level languages, programming became completely machine-independent and simpler. However, the need for better and faster code brought about the concept of object-oriented programming. An object-oriented program can be compared to the real-world scenario. Our entire world can be broadly classified into several classes and objects. Similarly, an object-oriented program involves classes and objects. For example, if human being is considered as a class, man and woman are instances of this class. By the same reason, man and woman are objects of the Human class.

The features of the object-oriented programming language include data abstraction, data encapsulation, polymorphism, and inheritance. In this chapter, you will look at these features in detail. You will also learn to implement object-orientation by using Ruby. In addition, you will learn how to use classes and objects and help Knowledge, Inc., a bookstore in the United States, to maintain its customer details. You will also use different kinds of variables provided by Ruby, such as class variables, to help identify the number of users who have visited the bookstore's Web site. You will use the inheritance feature of object orientation to display customer details with transactional details for Knowledge, Inc.

Features of Object Orientation

Object orientation has become a buzzword with many meanings. It is a design methodology, a paradigm, and a form of programming. As a design methodology, we can use object-oriented techniques to design software systems. But it is more than a design methodology, it is a whole new way of thinking about problems. Object-oriented design allows us to think about the actual, real world entities of the problem we are attempting to solve. Beginning the design with concepts from the real-world problem domain allows the same concepts to be carried over to implementation, making the design and implementation cycle more seamless. Once a design has been conceived, a programming language can be chosen for implementation.

The benefits of using the object-oriented approach are:

- Easier analysis and design.
- Code reuse
- Ease of maintenance and enhancement
- Fewer and shorter iterations

The two components of object-orientation are *classes* and *objects.* You may want to know what classes and objects are. A class is a broad term to describe a group of data members. Take the example of any vehicle. It comprises wheels, horsepower, and fuel or gas tank capacity. The characteristics of a vehicle can also include the number of occupants that the vehicle can accommodate. These characteristics form the data members of the class Vehicle. You can differentiate one vehicle from the other with the help of these characteristics. A vehicle can also have certain functions, such as halting, driving, and speeding. Even these functions form the data members of the class Vehicle. You can, therefore, define a class as a combination of characteristics and functions. A class Vehicle can be defined as:

```
Class Vehicle
{
Number no_of_wheels
Number horsepower
Characters type_of_tank
Number Capacity
 Function speeding
 {
 }
 Function driving
 {
 }
 Function halting
 {
 }
}
```

By assigning different values to these data members, you can form several instances of the class Vehicle. For example, an airplane has three wheels, horsepower of 1,000, fuel as the type of tank, and a capacity of 100 liters. In the same way, a car has four wheels, horsepower of 200, gas as the type of tank, and a capacity of 25 litres. Therefore, you can say that airplane and car are objects of the class Vehicle. In this way, you can instantiate several objects of a class.

Because an object-oriented programming language is very much like the real world, it also supports features such as data encapsulation, data abstraction, polymorphism, and inheritance. Let us look at each of these features in detail. One more important concept we will discuss is access control.

Data Encapsulation

While driving a car, does the driver need to think about what happens in the engine either while stepping up the acceleration or while applying the brake? The truth is that the driver need not be concerned with the functioning of the internal mechanisms of the car. It could be said that the driver remains unaware about the internal mechanisms of the car. In the same way, the data in a class cannot be accessed from outside the class. This is called *data encapsulation*. It is also termed data hiding.

Data Abstraction

From the preceding example, you know that the driver need not be bothered about the internal mechanisms of the car because that data is hidden from him. However, he still has access to the steering wheel, the accelerator, the brake, the seats, and various other parts of the car. This is termed as data abstraction. The data of the class, which is accessible after some data is hidden, is termed *data abstraction*.

Inheritance

If an automobile manufacturer wants to produce a new model of a car, does it go about creating a car from scratch or does it build on the existing functionality? The automobile manufacturer will build on the existing features because the basic functions of a car remain the same. Therefore, the new model consists of the basic characteristics and functionality. This is termed *inheritance* where the characteristics pass on from the parent class to the child class.

Polymorphism

Polymorphism simply means existing in different forms. A class, which is inherited from another class, will exhibit all the characteristics of its parent class. Now if you have identical data members or data members with the same name in these classes, that particular data member will exhibit polymorphism. For example, you have a method, Driving, in the class Vehicle and the class Car that is inherited from the class Vehicle also explicitly defines another method by the name Driving. The method Driving exhibits polymorphism.

Identifying the Features of Object Orientation

Problem Statement

Knowledge, Inc. comprises two departments, Accounts and Library. The Accounts Department decides on the reading charges for a book. It also decides on the number of days for which a book can be issued to a customer. The Accounts Department decides whether the customer should be fined or not after a book is returned. The Library section is in charge of the maintenance of books, updating the collection with the latest books, and issuing books. The Library section can also decide on the reading charge of the book and the number of days for issuing the book.

However, the levying of a penalty is the prerogative of the Accounts section. The Library section does not have anything to do with levying penalty. In addition to these functions, both departments perform a common function, which is appraising employees. The Accounts section has 30 employees, and these employees operate 20 computers among themselves. The Library section has 25 people and five computers. Identify the classes, characteristics, and functions of these classes. Identify the various features of object orientation supported in the case study.

Task List

✔ **Identify the various classes.**
✔ **Identify the characteristics and functions of each class.**
✔ **Identify the inheritance feature.**
✔ **Identify the data encapsulation and data abstraction feature.**

Identify the Various Classes

Result

In the preceding example, you will examine the three broad classifications. There are three classes. Identify each class. One is class Department, the second class is Accounts, and the third class is Library.

```
Class Department
{
}
Class Accounts
{
}
Class Library
{
}
```

Identify the Characteristics and Functions of Each Class

Result

You will now examine the different characteristics and functions of each of these classes. The Accounts department and the Library Department perform certain unique functions and a common function, which is employee appraisals. The class Department will show the common function, employee appraisals. Both departments also show the same characteristics, which are the number of people and the number of computers. You will now learn to classify these characteristics and functions into each of these classes.

```
Class Department
{
Number no_of_people
Number no_of_computers
Function employee_appraisal
{
}
}
Class Accounts
{
Function reading_charge
{
}
Function return_date
{
}
Function levying_fine
{
}
}
Class Library
```

```
{
Function maintenance
{
}
Function issuing
{
}
Function updating
{
}
}
```

The Class Department shows the common characteristics, which are no_of_people and no_of_computers. It also shows the common function, which is employee_appraisal. The other two classes show their respective common functions.

Identify the Inheritance Feature

Result

As you have seen, the Class Department shows the common features of both classes. Therefore, you decide on the Class Department as the parent class and the two classes, Class Accounts and Class Library, as child classes. We can, therefore, say that the Class Accounts and the Class Library are inherited from their parent class, Department.

Identify the Data Encapsulation and Data Abstraction Feature

Result

The Library section can access the reading_charge function and return_date function of the Accounts class. However, it cannot access the levying_fine function of the Accounts class. Therefore, you can say that the levying_fine function is hidden or encapsulated from the Library class. The earlier case study supports data encapsulation in the form of the levying_fine function and data abstraction in the form of the reading_charge and return_date functions.

Implementing Object Orientation in Ruby

Problem Statement

Knowledge Inc. needs to keep track of all customer details, such as customer ID, customer name, and customer address. The company also wants to keep track of the number of customers.

You will now look at the tasks to solve the problem.

Task List

- ✔ **Create the identified class.**
- ✔ **Declare the initialize method.**
- ✔ **Declare the methods for displaying the details of the customer and the number of customers.**
- ✔ **Create two objects of the** `Customer` **class to check if the correct output is displayed.**
- ✔ **Save and execute the code.**

Create the Identified Class

To implement object-oriented programming by using Ruby, you need to first learn how to create objects and classes in Ruby.

Creating a `Class`

A class in Ruby always starts with the keyword `class` followed by the name of the class. The name should always be in initial capitals. The class `Customer` can be displayed as:

```
class Customer
end
```

You terminate a class by using the keyword end. All the data members in the class are between the class definition and the end keyword.Because the class has been defined, you will now define the class variable. Before defining the class variable, you will need to check out the different variables supported by Ruby.

Variables in a Class

Ruby provides four types of variables: local, global, instance, and class. Local variables are the variables that are defined in a method. Local variables are not available outside the method. On the other hand, instance variables are available across methods for any particular instance or object. Instance variables are unique for every object and are not available across several objects. That means that instance variables change from object to object. Instance variables are preceded by the at sign (@) followed by the variable name. Class variables are available across different objects. A class variable belongs to the class and is a characteristic of a class. They are preceded by the sign @@ and are followed by the variable name. All three variables are declared inside the class. Class variables are not available across classes. If you want to have a single variable, which is available across classes, you need to define a global variable. The global variables are always preceded by the dollar sign ($).

In relation to the different variables supported by Ruby, you need to determine why class variables should be used for the case study instead of any other variables. Each person who visits the site of Knowledge, Inc. has to enter customer details. These details are stored in the database. Each time the person creates his or her details, an instance of the `class Customer` is created. Therefore, using the class variable `@@no_of_customers`, you can determine the number of objects that are being created. This enables in deriving the number of customers.

```
class Customer
@@no_of_customers=0
end
```

Declare the Initialize Method

Before learning about the initialize method, you need to know the reason for using such a method for a class. Here, you will learn about two concepts. One is creating objects by a simple method, and the other is creating objects by passing parameters.

Creating Objects the Simple Way

Objects are instances of the class. You will now learn how to create objects of a class in Ruby. You can create objects in Ruby by using the method new

of the class. This method new is a unique type of method, which is predefined in the Ruby library. The new method belongs to the class methods.
You will learn more about class methods in the subsequent chapters. We can
create two objects cust1 and cust2 of the class Customer as shown
below.

```
cust1 = Customer. new
cust2 = Customer. New
```

Here, cust1 and cust2 are the names of two objects. You write the
object name followed by the equal to sign (=) after which the class name
will follow. Then, the dot operator and the keyword new will follow.

Creating Objects by Passing Parameters to the new Method

You learned how to create objects by using the new method. How will you
initialize the properties of the object at the time of its creation? In Ruby,
this can be done easily by passing parameters to the new method. You will
now learn to do this. You create two objects, cust1 and cust2, by using
parameters.

```
cust1=Customer.new("0001", "Valerie", "22, New State road, Atlanta")
cust2=Customer.new("0002", "Esmer", "10, New Empire road, Texas")
```

Here, we see that the cust1 object is created by passing three parameters: 0001, Valerie, and 22, New State road, Atlanta. The cust2
object is created by passing 0002, Esmer, and 10, New Empire road,
Texas as the parameters.

When you plan to declare the new method with parameters, you need to
declare the method initialize at the time of the class creation. This
initialize method is a special type of method, which will be executed
when the new method of the class is called with parameters.

We can declare the code as follows:

```
class Customer
@@no_of_customers=0
def initialize(id, name, addr)
            @cust_id=id
            @cust_name=name
            @cust_addr=addr
    end
    end
```

In the above code, you declare the initialize method with id, name,
and addr as local variables. In the initialize method, you pass on the

values of these local variables to the instance variables @cust_id, @cust_name, and @cust_addr. Why do you need to pass the values from the local variables to instance variables? The reason is that the local variables hold the values that are passed along with the new method. In short, these local variables hold the characteristics of the object that is created. The unique characteristics of an object are always stored in instance variables.

Declare the Methods for Displaying the Details of the Customer and the Number of Customers

Members in a Class

The data members in a class include variables and functions. In Ruby, functions are called methods. Each method in a class starts with the keyword def followed by the method name. The method name should always be in lowercase letters. You end a method in Ruby by using the keyword end. You will now learn how to define a simple method.

```
class Sample
def samp
            statement 1
            statement 2
end
end
```

In the above example, statement 1 and statement 2 are part of the body of the method samp inside the class Sample. You will learn to add some logical statements instead of only statement 1 and statement 2. You start with a simple output statement, such as puts. The puts statement is used to display content on the display device. There are some other commands such as printf that can also be used for output. Right now, you will learn only to display a statement on our display device.

```
puts "Hello world"
```

The code displays Hello world on to the screen followed by a new blank line. The statement, which needs to be displayed, should always be enclosed in double quotation marks.

If you want to display the values of variables on the screen, you can use the following piece of code:

```
i=5
puts i
```

To display the variables, you write the variable name after the keyword puts. This piece of code will produce the output 5 followed by a blank line. You will now define the class Sample:

```
class Sample
def samp
      puts "This is sample code"
end
end
```

How will you pass parameters to the method? To do this, you declare the function with a local variable.

You have learned how to declare methods. For your case study, you will declare two methods, displayDetails and total_no_of_customers. The displayDetails method will display the details of the customer while the total_no_of_customers method will display the total number of customers at Knowledge, Inc.

```
class Customer
@@no_of_customers=0
def initialize(id, name, addr)
          @cust_id=id
          @cust_name=name
          @cust_addr=addr
end

def displayDetails()
          puts "Customer id #@cust_id"
          puts "Customer name #@cust_name"
          puts "Customer address #@cust_addr"
end
def total_no_of_customers()
          @@no_of_customers += 1
          puts "Total number of customers: #@@no_of_customers"
end
end
```

The displayDetails method contains three puts statements displaying the Customer ID, the Customer name, and the Customer address. The puts statement

```
puts "Customer id #@cust_id"
```

will display the text Customer id followed by the value of the variable @cust_id in a single line. When you want to display the text and the value of the instance variable in a single line, you need to precede the variable name with the hash symbol (#) in the `puts` statement. The text and the instance variable along with the hash symbol (#) should be enclosed in double quotation marks.

The second method, `total_no_of_customers`, is a method that contains the class variable `@@no_of_customers`. The expression `@@no_of_customers+=1` adds 1 to the variable `no_of_customers` each time the method `total_no_of_customers` is called. In this way, you will always have the total number of customers in the class variable.

Create Two Objects of the Customer Class to Check if the Correct Output Is Displayed

You will now create two objects, `cust1` and `cust2`, for the `Customer` class.

```
cust1=Customer.new("0001", "Valerie", "22, New State road, Atlanta")
cust2=Customer.new("0002", "Esmer", "10, New Empire road, Texas")
```

Here, we create two objects of the `Customer` class as `cust1` and `cust2` and pass the necessary parameters with the `new` method. The `initialize` method is invoked, and the necessary properties of the object are initialized.

Once the objects are created, you need to call the methods of the class by using the two objects. If you want to call a method or any data member, you write the following:

```
cust1.displayDetails()
cust1.total_no_of_customers()
```

The object name should always be followed by a dot, which is in turn followed by the method name or any data member. We have seen how to call the two methods by using the `cust1` object. Using the the `cust2` object, you can call both methods as shown below:

```
cust2.displayDetails()
cust2.total_no_of_customers()
```

Save and Execute the Code

It is always better to use Notepad or Editpad while working in Windows. After writing the code, save the file as the **Customer.rb** file. To execute the code, type `Ruby Customer.rb` at the command prompt. (See Figure 2.1.)

```
C:\Ruby>ruby Customer.rb
Customer id 0001
Customer name Valerie
Customer address 22, New state road, Atlanta
Total number of customers : 1
Customer id 0002
Customer name Esmer
Customer address 10, New Empire road, Texas
Total number of customers : 2
```

Figure 2.1   The case study example.

Inheritance

The concept of inheritance makes object-oriented programming language closer to reality. In the real world, features are handed down from one generation to another. In the same way, in object orientation, one class inherits features from its parent class. This parent class can be called super class or base class. The inherited class will be called the child class. What do you understand by the statement that features are inherited by one class from another class? This means that each data member of the parent class becomes a data member of the child class. A child class, in addition, can have its own data members. This will be explained with an example.

For example, every animal has certain common characteristics, such as eyes, legs, ears, and tail. However, does this mean that all animals are the same? The answer is no. You know that there are animals that differ massively in food habits. Even birds and human beings are closely related to the animals. They can also be classified as animals. Therefore, all the animals have certain characteristics that are common and certain characteristics that are special. Animals are the super class and the different kinds of animals are the child class. You will learn how to implement inheritance in Ruby. For example, take the sample code as shown below.

```ruby
class Vehicle
  def driving
      puts "Every vehicle can drive"
  end
end
class Plane < Vehicle
  def flying
      puts "Only planes can fly"
  end
end
objPlane=Plane.new
objPlane.driving
objPlane.flying
```

The Vehicle class consists of the method driving, and the Plane class shows the method flying. If you want to make the Plane class as a child class of the Vehicle class, then write as follows:

```
Child class < Parent class
```

In the above example it will become:

```
Class Plane < Vehicle
```

As a result, you can even call the driving method by using a Plane object. This is despite the fact that the method does not belong to the Plane class. This is called the power of inheritance, which eliminates data redundancy to a great extent.

There is another important concept in object orientation, called access control.

Access Control

It is very important to determine how much class you want to expose to the outside world. What do you mean exactly by exposing a class? Each class has data members in the form of variables and methods. In object orientation, you can restrict the access to these data members from outside the class by specifying access controls. In Ruby, you have three types of access controls: public, private, and protected. What is the difference between public, private, and protected access controls? When you specify a data member as public, this particular data member can be accessed from outside the class. By default, all the data members in Ruby are public except the initialize method. The initialize method is always private.

When you make a data member in a class as protected, that particular data member can be accessed only by those classes that inherit from this class. This implies that only the child classes can access the protected data members of the parent class. The rest of the world cannot access it. Now, private, as the name suggests, is private to the class. This particular data member can be accessed only from within the class. Not even the child classes can access the private data members of their parent. Now, you will see how to create these access controls in Ruby. Consider a class:

```
class Car
    def method1
    end
```

This `method1` by default is public. You can even write as:

```
Class Car
    public
    def method1
    end
end
```

To declare a protected or private member, replace the keyword `public` with an appropriate access control.

```
class Car
    protected
    def method1
    end
end
```

This will make `method1` protected. You have seen how to declare one data member as protected. How will you make three data members in a class protected?

```
class Car

    protected
    def method1
    end

    protected
    def method2
    end

    protected
    def method3
    end
end
```

The above method becomes a little tedious if there are large numbers of data members in your class. Here, Ruby helps you by allowing you to declare the access specifier only once. All the data members following this particular data member will have the same level of access. You will declare the above class in a different way.

```
class Car
    protected
    def method1
    end

    def method2
```

```
        end

        def method3
        end
    end
```

Now, if you declare your class in this way, all three methods become protected. The method method1 is declared as protected. All the data members
following this method will become protected unless stated otherwise. You
will now see one more example to make the preceding statement clear.

Consider that you want to declare a class with three protected methods, two private methods, and one public method. See how Ruby
makes this simpler for you.

You will first declare the public method, followed by two private
methods, and then the last three protected methods.

```
class Car
    def method1
    end
    private
    def method2
    end
    def method3
    end
    protected
    def method4
    end
    def method5
    end
    def method6
    end
end
```

In the above example, you use all three access specifiers. Before method1
no access specifier is mentioned. Hence, by default, it becomes a public
member. A private access specifier is mentioned before method2. This
method, therefore, becomes a private method. Now, all the methods following this method will be private unless stated otherwise. Before method3,
there is no access specifier. Hence, method3 also becomes private. Now
before method4, the protected access specifier is mentioned. Hence,
method4 becomes protected. Now, all the methods following method4
will be protected unless stated otherwise. Before method5 and method6,
there are no access specifiers mentioned. Hence, method5 and method6
become protected.

You will now look at implementing inheritance in your case study.

Problem Statement

Knowledge, Inc. needs to keep track of the number of times a particular customer has visited its site and the total amount of purchases he has made to date. The transaction details should be displayed with the customer details.

Let us look at the tasks to solve the problem.

Task List

- ✔ **Create a child class** `Transaction` **of the parent class** `Customer` **and declare the initialize method.**
- ✔ **Call the relevant methods for displaying the customer details and the transaction details.**
- ✔ **Save and execute the code.**

Create a Child Class Called Transaction of the Parent Class Customer

Result

You will first display the `class Customer`. Then, you will create the `Transaction` class. The `Transaction` class will inherit all the features of the `Customer` class.

```
class Customer
@@no_of_customers=0

    def initialize(id, name, addr)
            @cust_id=id
            @cust_name=name
            @cust_addr=addr
    end

    def displayDetails()
            puts "Customer id #@cust_id"
            puts "Customer name #@cust_name"
            puts "Customer address #@cust_addr"
    end

    def total_no_of_customers()
            @@no_of_customers += 1
            puts "Total number of customers: #@@no_of_customers"
    end
end
```

This is the `Customer` class, which you created earlier. Now, you will create the `Transaction` class.

```
class Transaction < Customer
    def initialize(id, name, addr, no_of_times, amount)
            super (id, name, addr)
            @no_of_times=no_of_times
            @amount=amount
    end
    def tranDetails()
puts "Number of times you have visited is #@no_of_times"
puts "Total purchases at this site made by you: #@amount"
    end
end
```

The above statement class `Transaction` < `Customer` clearly states that the `Transaction` class is a child class of the `Customer` class. If you look at the initialize method of this class, you will see that the three parameters `id`, `name`, and `addr` that are passed to it are the same as those passed to the `initialize` method of the `Customer` class. Therefore, the best thing would be to pass these three variables to the `Customer` class. There is a method called `super`, which allows you to do that. You can call the `super` method with the parameters you want to pass. This `super` method will in turn invoke the `initialize` method of the `Customer` class. The other two local variables `no_of_times` and `amount` would be stored in the instance variables in this class itself. The `tranDetails` method displays the number of times the customer has visited the site and the total amount of purchases made by the customer at the site.

Call the Relevant Methods for Displaying the Customer Details as Well as the Transaction Details

Result

You will first create the two objects of the class `Transaction` by using the new method.

```
cust1_tran=Transaction.new("0001", "Valerie", "22, New State road,
Atlanta", 5, 500)
cust2_tran=Transaction.new("0002", "Esmer", "10, New Empire road,
Texas", 10, 400)
```

Now, the `displayDetails` method is also available to the `Transaction` class object. Because you need to display the Customer ID, the Customer name, the Customer address, the number of times the customer has visited the site, and the total amount of purchases made, you call both methods, displayDetails and tranDetails, by using the cust1_ tran and cust2_tran objects.

```
cust1_tran.displayDetails()
cust1_tran.tranDetails()
cust2_tran.displayDetails()
cust2_tran.tranDetails()
```

Save and Execute the Code

Save the file as a **Transaction.rb** file. To execute the code, type Ruby Transaction.rb at the command prompt. (See Figure 2.2.)

Until now, you have seen examples of single inheritance. However, everything in the real world cannot be explained on the basis of single inheritance. A class does not necessarily inherit all its features from one parent class only. For example, computers can be considered as an electronic device as well as a machine. In such situations, the child class will have more than one parent class. Such a feature is called *multiple inheritance*. Not all object-oriented programming languages support multiple inheritance. The language C++ directly supports multiple inheritance. Java does not support multiple inheritance directly but shows multiple inheritance partially by using interfaces. Similarly, Ruby also does not support multiple inheritance directly but shows multiple inheritance partially by using mixins. You will learn more about mixins later.

```
C:\Ruby>ruby Transaction.rb
Customer id 0001
Customer name Valerie
Customer address 22, New state road, Atlanta
Number of times you have visited is 5
Total purchases at this site made by you: 500
Customer id 0002
Customer name Esmer
Customer address 10, New Empire road, Texas
Number of times you have visited is 10
Total purchases at this site made by you: 400
```

Figure 2.2 The case study example.

Summary

In this chapter, you learned:

- The need for object orientation.
- You were introduced to classes and objects.
- You learned that the features of object orientation are data encapsulation, data abstraction, inheritance, and polymorphism.
- The different types of variables are local, global, class, and instance.
- You can create an object by using the `new` method.
- You can also create an object by using the `new` method with parameters.
- Finally, you learned about access control in Ruby by using `private`, `protected`, and `public`.

CHAPTER

3

Programming Basics

OBJECTIVES

In this chapter you will learn:
- To assign different data types to variables
- To declare arrays and hashes in Ruby
- To use ranges

Getting Started

Programming is all about data manipulation or actually playing with data. What does the term *programming* actually mean? In a broader sense, programming is nothing but copying or transferring selected data from one location to another. For example, transferring data from a Web site to a database is one type of programming. Today, programming deals more with displaying data in a particular format. This is the reason why there is a concept of front end and back end. For example, a computer game displays graphics in a particular manner within a specified time interval, giving the effect of animation. Similarly, network programming is concerned with transferring data over the network or virus programming, which involves writing code for deleting data and replacing it with junk data.

In programming, you often need to access memory either directly or indirectly. Some programming languages, such as C and C++, allow you to access memory directly, whereas other programming languages, such as Visual Basic and Java, do not. One common aspect across all programming languages is the use of variables to store data in memory. Therefore, variables play a big role in any form of programming.

What are variables? *Variables* are reserved memory locations. This means that when you declare a variable, what you actually do is reserve some space in memory. Who decides how much memory is to be reserved and what should be stored in this memory? These decisions are made by assigning data types to variables. Based on the data type of the variable, the compiler allocates memory and also decides what can be stored in reserved memory. Therefore, by assigning different data types to variables, you can store integers, decimals, or characters in these variables. Consider another situation in which you need to store a large amount of related data. One method is to declare multiple variables and then recall the names of all these variables. A simpler method is to use arrays or hashes in Ruby.

In this chapter you will learn how to use variables, arrays, and hashes in Ruby by using the Knowledge, Inc., case study. You will store and display customer details by using different variables. You also will learn to use arrays and hashes to store all the information about customers. Finally, you will learn about ranges and the various methods supported by ranges.

Datatypes

Problem Statement

Anya buys two fiction books, *Beyond 2020* and *The Arrival of Doomsday*. She also buys a book, *Mastering Ruby*. *Beyond 2020* costs $55.80, *The Arrival of Doomsday* costs $25, and *Mastering Ruby* costs $44.20. You need to calculate the total amount Anya has to pay Knowledge, Inc. You also need to display the details of the purchases that Anya made. The details include the names of the books, their prices, and the total amount. After displaying all the details, you need to show the messages "Goodbye Anya" and "Thanks for Purchasing Online."

Task List

✔ **Declare the variables to store the details.**

✔ **Write the code to display the details.**

✔ **Save and execute the code.**

✔ **Verify the output.**

Declare the Variables to Store the Details

The names of books consist of characters, and the prices of books consist of numbers. Let us examine how Ruby handles numbers and characters.

Numbers

The entire set of numbers can always be divided into two, integers and decimals. In the area of programming, decimals are also termed *floats*. In Ruby, every integer is stored as an object either of the class Fixnum or the class Bignum. The question that arises next is, When is a number stored as a Fixnum and when is it stored as a Bignum? The answer is whenever a number is within the range -2^{62} and $2^{62} - 1$, then it is stored as an object of the class Fixnum. Whenever a number is beyond this range, it is stored as an object of the class Bignum. Therefore, the classes Bignum and Fixnum are related to integers. All decimal numbers are stored as objects of the class Float. You can find out the datatype of a particular number by calling the method type. Consider the following examples:

Example 1:

```
a = 5
puts a.type
```

The output of this code is Fixnum.

Example 2:

```
a = 5.888
puts a.type
```

The output of this code is Float.

Example 3:

```
a = 9999999999
puts a.type
```

The output of this code is Bignum.

The number 9999999999 is not in the range -2^{62} and 2^{62} -1. Therefore, this number is stored as an object of the class Bignum.

Strings

The character handling in Ruby is done by using strings. A *string* is nothing but a group of characters. In Ruby, a string is always stored as an object of the class String. Strings are always enclosed within delimiters. Ruby supports both single and double quotes as delimiters. Two other types of delimiters that are supported by Ruby are %q and %Q. When using %q or %Q, the character following %q or %Q becomes the delimiter.

Consider the following examples:

Example 1:

```
c=%q(hello world)
```

Here the parentheses are the delimiters. Therefore, the variable c contains the string hello world.

Example 2:

```
c=%Q hello world
```

Here the space becomes the delimiter. Therefore, the variable c contains only hello because %Q is followed by a space. In addition, a space after the word hello causes the string to be stored in c as hello.

Example 3:

```
c=%qhelloworldh
```

Here the delimiter becomes the letter h, and the variable c contains all the characters in the string until the letter h is reached again. Therefore, the variable c contains elloworld. The letter h is ignored because it is the delimiter.

In the case study you will store the names and prices of the books in variables. You declare the variables as shown below:

```
fiction_book1="Beyond 2020"
fiction_book2="The Arrival of Doomsday"
computer_book1="Mastering Ruby"
cost_book1=55.80
cost_book2=25.00
cost_book3=44.20
```

You also declare a variable that stores the total amount for all the books:

```
total_cost = cost_book1+cost_book2+cost_book3
```

Because you need to display the user name, Anya, you declare a string variable to store the name:

```
name="Anya"
```

You also need to declare two string variables to store the text Goodbye Anya and Thanks for Purchasing Online:

```
text1="Goodbye Anya"
text2="Thanks for Purchasing Online"
```

Here you use double quotes as the string delimiter.

Write the Code to Display the Details

Let us look at the code to display the customer name, the details of the books, and the total amount of the sale:

```
puts "Name : #{name}"
puts "Book Name: #{fiction_book1}"+"   "+"Cost of the book1:
#{cost_book1}"
puts "Book Name: #{fiction_book2}"+"   "+"Cost of the book2:
#{cost_book2}"
puts "Book Name: #{computer_book1}"+"   "+"Cost of the book3:
#{cost_book3}"
puts "Total cost of the purchases: #{total_cost}"
```

You can see how the puts statement is used differently. Let us consider the first statement:

```
puts "Name : #{name}"
```

You use the puts statement as shown here when you want the text and the value of the variable in the same line. The output of this puts statement is:

```
Name : Anya
```

To get this output, you first write the text and then the hash (#) symbol followed by the variable name in curly braces. One thing you need to ensure is that the text along with the variable name is enclosed in double quotes. Now consider the second puts statement:

```
puts "Book Name: #{fiction_book1}"+"   "+"Cost of the book1:
#{cost_book1}"
```

Here you use the plus (+) operator if you want to concatenate strings. In the preceding statement, we concatenated the book name, three spaces, and the cost of the book.

To display the text Goodbye Anya and Thanks for Purchasing Online, you can write:

```
puts text1
puts text2
```

Verify the Output

Verify that all the values are displayed correctly and are in the proper format. Figure 3.1 shows the output.

Arrays, Hashes, and Ranges

Arrays

When you declare a variable, you reserve a memory location. However, for situations in which you need to store a large amount of related data, you use arrays. This helps to reduce the number of variable names you need to remember because all the memory locations belonging to an array can be

```
C:\Ruby>ruby Customer_anya.rb
Name : Anya
Book Name: Beyond 2020   Cost of the book1:  55.8
Book Name: The arrival of the Doomsday   Cost of the book2:  25.0
Book Name: Mastering Ruby   Cost of the book3: 44.2
Total cost of the purchases: 125.0
Goodbye Anya
Thanks for Purchasing Online
```

Figure 3.1 The screen output.

referenced by one name. How do you then differentiate one memory location from another? To access the individual elements of the array, you use an integer as the key. In Ruby, an array can contain a mixture of strings and numbers. Let us look at different ways to declare an array:

```
sample = ['Cat', 'Cow', 'Mouse']
```

We declared an array `sample` containing three elements: `Cat`, `Cow`, and `Mouse`. The elements of the array should always be enclosed in square brackets. Each element of the array should be separated by a comma. If you want to remove the commas and quotes, you can use the following statement:

```
sample = %w[Cat Cow Mouse]
```

You can even have an array containing a mixture of both strings and numbers as elements:

```
sample = [1,2,3,'Ken']
```

Ruby is a pure object-oriented language. Therefore, even an array is a class. The class `Array` supports many methods, which are predefined in the Ruby library. Let us look at some of them.

The Method new

You can create an array by using the method `new` of the class `Array`. This is another method of creating an array:

```
sample = Array.new
```

After the array is created, you need to assign elements to the array. This can be done as shown below:

```
sample[0]="Cat"
sample[1]="Cow"
sample[2]="Mouse"
```

The first element in the array always has the index value of zero. Therefore, `sample[0]` refers to the first element of that array:

```
sample[0]="Cat"
```

Here `Cat` is stored as the first element of the array:

```
sample[1]="Cow"
sample[2]="Mouse"
```

Using the preceding statements, `Cow` and `Mouse` become the second and third elements of the array, respectively.

The Method type

The method `type` displays the datatype of the variable:

```
puts sample.type
```

The output of this code is `Array`.

The Method length

The method `length` gives the number of elements in the array. Consider the following statement:

```
puts sample.length
```

The output is 3.

Hashes

Hashes are similar to arrays. In a *hash*, you declare two sets of elements. One set of elements is called *keys,* and the other set is called *values*. Using the keys, you can access the values in a hash. Therefore, you access the array elements by using integers, and you access the hash elements by using key elements. You will learn how to access hash elements later.

Ranges

A *range* is a series of numbers. The range of numbers from 20 to 25 includes 20, 21, 22, 23, 24, and 25. When you refer to the financial year of the company, it actually ranges within one year. Therefore, a range can be used in everything right from numbers, days, months, and years. Ruby also supports ranges in its own way. There are two types of range operators. One is a two-dot operator (. .), and the other is a three-dot operator (. . .). When do you use the two-dot operator, and when do you use the three-dot operator?

Let us see some examples. Suppose that you want a range of numbers between 1 and 100 with both 1 and 100 inclusive. You use the two-dot operator. You define:

```
range1 = 1..100
```

Now the variable `range1` will contain all the numbers between 1 and 100, both inclusive. The variable `range1` actually becomes an array.

In a similar manner, you also can define the range using the three-dot operator:

```
range2 = 1...100
```

However, here the `range2` variable will hold all the values between 1 and 100, except the higher value, 100.

There are certain functions, such as `max`, `min`, and `include`, that you can use with these ranges. Let us see how to use these functions.

The max Function

As the name suggests, this function gives the highest number in the range:

```
puts range1.max
```

The output of this code is `100`.

The min Function

As the name suggests, this function gives the lowest number in the range:

```
puts range1.min
```

The output of this code is `1`.

The include Function

The `include` function can be used to check whether a particular number is within a range or not. The `include` function always will return a true or false. For example:

```
range1.include? (6)
```

This code returns true because `range1` contains numbers from 1 to 100.

You saw how different functions are used with a range. What if you want to display the full range in the form of a list? Here you will use another function, to a.

The to a Method

```
range1 = 1..100
puts range1.to_a
```

This code outputs the values 1 to 100 in a sequence as a list form. Or you can directly write:

```
range1 = (1..100).to_a
puts range1
```

 ## Problem Statement

The Sales Department of Knowledge, Inc., needs the daily sales report from the Web site for Thursday. On that day, five customers purchased books. You need to display the names of these customers. You also need to display the total purchases made by each of these customers. The names of the customers and the total purchases made are given in Table 3.1.

 ## Task List

☑ **Declare an array to store all the customer names.**
☑ **Write the code to display the customer names.**
☑ **Declare a hash of customers with the customer names as the key.**
☑ **Write the code to display the customer details.**
☑ **Save and execute the code.**
☑ **Verify the details.**

Table 3.1   The Sample Input

CUSTOMER NAMES	TOTAL PURCHASES
Ken	$234
William	$200
Catherine	$124.30
Steve	$148.30
Mark	$175

Declare an Array to Store All the Customer Names

You can declare an array by any of the methods discussed earlier. You will name the array `customer_array`.

```
customer_array = ['Ken', 'William', 'Catherine', 'Steve', 'Mark']
```

Write the Code to Display the Customer Names

To access the elements of the array `customer_array`, you can write the following code:

```
puts customer_array[0]
puts customer_array[1]
puts customer_array[2]
puts customer_array[3]
puts customer_array[4]
```

This provides all five elements of the array. You also can access the elements of the array by using negative values:

```
puts customer_array[-5]
puts customer_array[-4]
puts customer_array[-3]
puts customer_array[-2]
puts Customer_array[-1]
```

The zeroth element maps to the -5 element, the first element maps to the -4 element, and so on.

Declare a Hash of Customers with Customer Names as the Key

Let's look at how to declare a hash:

```
Customer_hash = {
'Ken' => 234,
'William' => 200,
'Catherine' => 124.30,
'Steve' => 148.30,
'Mark' => 175
}
```

`customer_hash` has five elements. The customer names become the key. Just as in an array, you can use an integer as the key to access the array elements. Here you use the customer names as the key to access the total purchases made. While declaring the hash, you need to map the key elements you want to access using the => (equal to and greater than) operator.

You can map the user Mark with 175 using the following statement:

```
'Mark'=>175
```

One more important point you need to remember is that a hash can be used only with curly braces ({}) and not with square brackets ([]).

Write the Code to Display the Customer Details

```
puts customer hash['Ken']
puts customer hash['William']
puts customer hash['Catherine']
puts customer hash['Steve']
puts customer hash['Mark']
```

Save and Execute the Code

Save the code as customer details.rb, and then execute the code from the command prompt.

Verify the Details

Verify whether all the values are displayed correctly and are in the proper format.

Summary

In this chapter you learned that:

- Integers are stored as objects of class Fixnum or Bignum.
- Decimals are stored as objects of class Float and characters are stored as objects of class String.
- Arrays are groups of continuous memory locations with a single name.

- Array elements can be accessed by using an integer as the key.

- Hashes are similar to arrays and that hashes use two sets of elements.

- One set of hash elements is called a *key* and the other set is called a *value*.

Using these key elements, you can access the value elements. Ranges can be useful, as can the various methods supported by ranges.

CHAPTER

4

Control Structures, Blocks, and Expressions

OBJECTIVES

In this chapter you will learn to:

- ✔ Use control structures
- ✔ Understand and implement blocks and iterators
- ✔ Use regular expressions

Getting Started

Decision making is one of the key aspects you need to consider in programming. It is possible that your code may have two or more conditions specified. In such a situation, your code should be programmed to carry out the correct steps depending on the conditions satisfied. In most of the programming languages, you can write decision-making statements by using `if..else` statements. Only the syntax changes in different programming languages. You will learn to write `if..else` statements in Ruby. Now consider a different situation in which you want to display all the elements of an array. If the array has 100 elements, then you need to write the `puts` statement 100 times. This amounts to a lot of unnecessary and unwanted code. Programming languages provide looping structures that help you to tackle such situations. You will learn about two looping structures in Ruby, the `while` loop and the `for` loop.

Nowadays, systems are highly automated and are complicated to create. The code that makes up these systems runs into a huge number of lines. Therefore, it has become important to create well-structured code. What happens if one of the programmers constructing a particular code suddenly quits the company? Unless the code has meaningful variables and functions that are defined and is structured properly, a new programmer will have a lot of difficulty understanding the code. Most of the programming languages include functionality with which you can structure code. Ruby provides blocks to structure code.

One of the ways to access array (or hash) elements is to use looping structures such as the `while` loop and the `for` loop. Another way to access the elements of an array or a hash is by using iterators. *Iterators* are special methods that can be used to access elements one by one. In this chapter you will learn about the different iterators used in Ruby.

You learned about strings in Chapter 3. Strings consist of a group of characters in a particular sequence or pattern. These characters can be any letter from *a* through *z* or from *A* through *Z* or can be any digit from 0 through 9. These characters also can be any of the special characters, such as {, }, (,), *, &, ^, #, $, |, or \. What if you want to find a particular character or sequence of characters in a string? For example, you may have a string, `Hello Everybody. Good Morning! Today is 22nd December (Tuesday)`. Now this string consists of nine words: `Hello`, `Everybody`, `Good`, `Morning`, `Today`, `is`, `22nd`, `December`, and `Tuesday`. The string also consists of special characters, such as a period (`.`), a space, an exclamation mark (`!`), and parentheses (`( )`). Suppose that you want to find the word `body` in this string. Then you need to specify the word `body` in between two slashes — `/body/` — and then compare it with the string by using any of the conditional statements. This word becomes a regular expression. Therefore, you can define a *regular expression* as a sequence of characters or a pattern of characters found in a string. Regular expressions are always enclosed within two slashes.

Control Structures

We can implement control structures in Ruby by using the `if..else`, `while`, and `for` statements.

The if .. else Loop

Unlike other programming languages, which use braces in `if..else` statements, Ruby uses the keyword `end`. Let's see how to implement it:

```
if Condition 1
     Statement 1
     Statement 2
else
     Statement 3
     Statement 4
end
```

Going by this syntax, if `condition 1` is satisfied, then `statement 1` and `statement 2` are executed. If `condition 1` becomes false, then `statement 3` and `statement 4` are executed. You always terminate the `if` statement by using the keyword `end`. There is also another type of `if` statement. This is the `if. . .elsif. . .else` statement:

```
if Condition 1
     Statement 1
     Statement 2
elsif Condition 2
     Statement 3
     Statement 4
else
     Statement 5
     Statement 6
end
```

If `Condition 1` is not true, then control goes to the `elsif` statement. If `Condition 2` is also not satisfied, then control goes to the `else` statement. We will look at samples of codes for both types of statements:

```
count = 10
if count==10
     puts "Count is equal to 10"
else
     puts "Count is not equal to 10"
end
```

In this example, the condition is whether the count variable is equal to 10 or not. Here you can see that there are two types of equals operators being used. One is single equals (=), and the other is double equals (==). The single equals operator is an assignment operator. The assignment operator assigns a value to a variable. Therefore:

```
count = 10
```

assigns the value 10 to the variable count.

The double equals (==) operator is always used in conditional statements to check the condition. Therefore:

```
count == 10
```

checks whether or not the count variable has the value 10.

Let's see the code for the `if..elsif..else` statement:

```
if count<10
     puts "Count is less than 10"
elsif count>=10 and count<=100
     puts "Count is between 10 and 100"
else
     puts "Count is greater than 100"
end
```

In this code, you check whether the value of count is less than 10, between 10 and 100, or greater than 100. The condition of less than 10 is checked by using the lesser than (<) operator. The condition of between 10 and 100 is checked by using two condition statements joined by the keyword and. One of the two condition statements checks for greater than or equal to 10 by using the greater than or equal to (>=) operator, and the other checks for lesser than or equal to 100 by using the lesser than or equal to (<=) operator. Only when both the conditions are true is the statement `puts "Count is between 10 and 100"` executed. Even if one of the conditions is false, then control goes to the `else` statement, and then `puts "Count is greater than 100"` is executed.

There is another way in which you can represent an `if` statement. Let us check out how to write a simple code both ways:

First method:

```
count = 10
if count==10
     puts "Count is equal to 10"
else
     puts "Count is not equal to 10"
end
```

The same code can be written in the second method as follows:

```
count = 10
if count==10 then puts "Count is equal to 10" else puts "Count is not
equal to 10" end
```

In the second method, you can write the entire `if else` statement in one line as a sentence. The only thing you need to remember is you should add the `then` keyword.

NOTE In the first method you can also use the `then` keyword but it is optional.

There is one more control structure, `unless`, which is similar to the `if` statement. The `unless` statement also uses the optional `else` like the `if` statement. Let us check out a sample code.

```
count = 10
unless count==10
     puts "Count is not equal to 10"
else
puts "Count is equal to 10"

end
```

The output of this code is:

```
Count is equal to 10
```

From the above code, you can infer that the `if` and `unless` statements work exactly the same way.

The `while` Loop

Loops are used when you want to execute a piece of code repeatedly. If you want to display an asterisk five times, then write `puts  "*"` five times. However, you can do the same by using a `while` loop, as shown below:

```
i=0
while i<5
     puts "*"
     i=i+1
end
```

This displays the output * five times in different lines on the screen. Therefore, the `while` loop syntax is:

```
while condition
     statement 1
     statement 2
end
```

All the statements between the statement `while condition` and the keyword `end` become the `while` loop.

Let's look at the code in detail. First, you initialize a `counter i=0`. Then you come to the `while` loop. The `while` loop has a condition that checks whether `i` is less than 5. Only when this condition is satisfied are the statements in the `while` loop executed.

Because `i=0`, the condition `i<5` becomes true, and the statements in the `while` loop are executed. The last statement in the `while` loop is:

```
i=i+1
```

This statement increases the value of the counter `i` by one. Then the condition is checked again. Because `i=1`, the condition `i<5` again becomes true. Then the counter is again increased by one, and the condition is checked. This continues until the counter reaches the value 5. When the value of the counter becomes 5, the condition `i<5` becomes false, and the control comes out of the `while` loop.

This is how the `while` loop is implemented in most of the programming languages, including Ruby. However, with Ruby things can always be done in a better and easier manner. The preceding four statements of the `while` loop can be represented in a single line as follows:

```
5.times{puts "*"}
```

Wow! Such a simple syntax! This is plain English. Just looking at the statement you know what will be the output.

The for Loop

To use the `for` loop in Ruby, you need to define a range; that is:

```
for i in 0..10
      puts "*"
end
```

Here we have defined the range `0..10`. The statement `for i in 0..10` will allow `i` to take values in the range from 0 to 10 (including 10). And even the `for` loop also is terminated with the keyword `end`.

Problem Statement

The customer names of Knowledge, Inc., are stored in an array, `Customer_array`. A hash, `Customer_hash`, stores the names of customers as the key and the types of books they are interested in as the values.

Management is planning to introduce some more fiction books in the store. Therefore, it needs to know the names of customers who have purchased fiction books in the past. You need to store the names of these customers in a separate array. Table 4.1 shows such an array.

Task List

- ✔ **Identify the array and hash of customers.**
- ✔ **Write the code to store the names of customers.**
- ✔ **Write the code to display the elements of the new array.**
- ✔ **Save and execute the code.**

Identify the Array and Hash of Customers

You will declare an array, Customer_array, to store the customers' names and a hash, Customer_hash, to store the customers' names and their choices of books:

```
customer_array = ['Ken','William','Catherine','Mark','Steve','Sam']
customer_hash = {
'Ken' => 'Fiction',
'William' => 'Mystery',
'Catherine' => 'Computer',
'Mark' => 'Fiction',
'Steve' => 'Sports',
'Sam' => 'Fiction'

}
```

Table 4.1 Customer Array

CUSTOMER NAMES	TYPE OF BOOKS
Ken	Fiction
William	Mystery
Catherine	Computer
Mark	Fiction
Steve	Sports
Sam	Fiction

Write the Code to Store the Names of Customers

You will first declare a new array:

```
customer_array2= Array.new
```

You will display the names of customers who are interested in fiction books and store the names in a separate array:

```
j=0
for i in 0...customer_array.length
    if customer_hash[customer_array[i]]=='Fiction'
            puts "#{customer_array[i]} has brought fiction books"
            customer_array2[j]=customer_array[i]
            j=j+1
    end
end
```

You have two arrays, `customer_array` and `customer_array2`. The `customer_array2` array stores the names of all customers who are interested in fiction books. You need to use two counters, `i` and `j`. The variable `i` is the counter for `customer_array`, and `j` is the counter for `customer_array2`. As stated earlier, the hash `customer_hash` has customers' names as the key and the types of books as its values. Therefore, in the `if` statement, that is:

```
if customer_hash[customer_array[i]]=='Fiction'
```

the elements of the array `customer_array` become the key for the hash `customer_hash`. Then, for each array element, the value of the hash is checked. If the value is `Fiction`, then the corresponding customer name is displayed on the screen and also stored in the new array, `customer array2`.

Write the Code to Display the Elements of the New Array

```
i=0
while i < customer_array2.length
    puts "The customers of fiction books are #{customer_array2[i]}"
    i=i+1
end
```

This code displays the elements of the new array.

```
D:\Wiley\Codes>ruby looping.rb
Ken has bought fiction books
Mark has bought fiction books
Sam has bought fiction books
The customers of fiction books are Ken
The customers of fiction books are Mark
The customers of fiction books are Sam
```

Figure 4.1 The screen output.

Save and Execute the Code

Save the code as `looping.rb,` and execute it at the command prompt.

Verify the Output

Verify whether the elements of the new array have all customer names belonging to the `Fiction` category (Figure 4.1).

Blocks and Regular Expressions

You use blocks mainly to structure programs. A *block* consists of chunks of code. You assign a name to a block. The code in the block is always enclosed within braces (`{}`). A block is always invoked from a function with the same name as that of the block. This means that if you have a block with the name `test`, then you use the function `test` to invoke this block. You invoke a block by using the `yield` statement. You will learn to invoke a block by using a simple `yield` statement. You will also learn to use a `yield` statement with parameters for invoking a block. You will check the sample code with both types of `yield` statements.

The yield Statement

Let's look at an example of the `yield` statement:

```
def test
    puts "You are in the method"
    yield
    puts "You are again back to the method"
    yield
end
test {puts "You are in the block"}
```

The output of this code is:

```
You are in the method
You are in the block
You are again back to the method
You are in the block
```

The code consists of a method called `test` that invokes the block test. Both the method name and the block name should be the same. First, the statement `puts "You are in the method"` will be executed. Then the `yield` statement will transfer control from the method to the block. The block, which consists of only one statement, `puts "You are in the block"`, will be executed. After this, control is transferred to the next statement (the statement following the `yield` statement) in the method. Finally, control is transferred back to the block because there is another `yield` statement.

Passing Parameters with the yield Statement

You also can pass parameters with the `yield` statement. Let's look at how:

```
def test
        yield 5
        puts "You are in the method test"
        yield 100
end
test {|i| puts "You are in the block #{i}"}
```

The output of this code will be:

```
You are in the block 5
You are in the method test
You are in the block 100
```

In the preceding code, the `yield` statement is written followed by parameters. You can even pass more than one parameter. In the block, you place a variable between two vertical lines (| |) to accept the parameters. Therefore, in the preceding code, the `yield 5` statement passes the value 5 as a parameter to the `test` block. Now look at the following statement:

```
test {|i| puts "You are in the block #{i}"}
```

Here the value 5 is received in the variable i. Now observe the following `puts` statement:

```
puts "You are in the block #{i}"
```

The output of this `puts` statement is:

```
You are in the block 5
```

If you want to pass more than one parameters, then the `yield` statement becomes:

```
yield a, b
```

and the block is:

```
test {|a, b| statement}
```

The parameters will be separated by commas.

Iterators

Iterators are nothing but methods supported by collections. Objects that store a group of data members are called *collections*. In Ruby, arrays and hashes can be termed *collections*. Iterators return all the elements of a collection, one after the other. We will be discussing two iterators here, `each` and `collect`. Let's look at these in detail.

each

The `each` iterator returns all the elements of an array or a hash. Check the output of this code:

```
a = [1,2,3,4,5]
a.each {| i | puts i}
```

The output of this code will be

```
1
2
3
4
5
```

You always associate the `each` iterator with a block. It returns each value of the array, one by one, to the block. The value is stored in the variable `i` and then displayed on the screen.

collect

The `collect` iterator returns all the elements of a collection. The `collect` method need not always be associated with a block. The `collect` method returns the entire collection, regardless of whether it is an array or a hash. We will first implement the `collect` method without a block.

```
a = [1,2,3,4,5]
b = Array.new
b = a.collect
puts b
```

In this code, you have an array, a, that has five elements. You call the `collect` method of the array. The output of the method also will be an array. Therefore, you create another array, b, and store the output of the `collect` method of array a in array b. Then you can display array b. This way you can do copying using the `collect` method. However, the `collect` method is not the right way to do copying between arrays. There is another method called a `clone`.

```
a = [1,2,3,4,5]
b = a.clone
puts b
```

Using the `clone` method is the actual way of copying between arrays. Now, let us implement the `collect` method with a block.

```
a = [1,2,3,4,5]
b = a.collect{|x| 10*x}
puts b
```

You normally use the `collect` method when you want to do something with each of the values to get the new array. For example, this code produces an array b containing 10 times each value in a.

Problem Statement

The names of the customers of Knowledge, Inc., are stored in the array `customer_array`. The array elements are as follows:

```
customer_array = %w [Anya Ken William Mark Steve]
```

Demonstrate the use of blocks and iterators and display the names of the customers.

Task List

✔ **Write the code for the block to display the array elements.**
✔ **Demonstrate the use of iterators.**
✔ **Save and execute the code.**
✔ **Verify the output.**

Write the Code for the Block to Display the Array Elements

You will declare the array `customer_array` as a global variable so that you can access it both inside and outside the methods.

```
$customer_array = %w[Anya Ken William Mark Steve]
```

Now you declare a method `customer_names` from which you can call the block by using the `yield` statement. The code will be as follows:

```
$customer_array = %w[Anya Ken William Mark Steve]
def customer_names
for i in 0...$customer_array.length
yield $customer_array[i]
end
end
customer_names { |name| puts "Customer Name: #{name}"}
```

In this code, the `for` loop is used to access each element of the array. From the `for` loop, the `yield` statement passes the elements of the array one by one as parameters to the block. Let's consider the block now. The block receives the array elements in the variable `name`, and the `puts` statement outputs the value of this variable. Note that the `customer_array` variable is a global variable. Therefore, whenever you need to refer to this variable, you need to precede the variable with a dollar ($) sign.

Demonstrate the Use of Iterators

Let's first use the `clone` method and copy all the elements of the `customer_array` into another array, `customer_array2`. Then, using the `each` iterator, display all the elements of `customer_array2`.

```
customer_array2=$customer_array.clone
customer_array2.each{|name| puts "Customers are #{name}"}
```

The clone method accesses each element of customer_array and transfers it to customer_array2. Then, using the each iterator, you can access all the elements of customer_array2.

Save and Execute the Code

Save the code as block.rb, and execute it from the command prompt.

Verify the Output

Verify whether elements of both the arrays are displayed and are the same (Figure 4.2).

Let's now look at regular expressions.

Regular Expressions

Before you use regular expressions, you need to understand the various types of syntax used to represent them. Table 4.2 describes the types of syntax.

Using the conventions noted in Table 4.2, you can form your own regular expressions and use them to search for a pattern of characters in a string. Let's examine some patterns of characters:

```
Pattern1 = /Perl/
Pattern2 = /\d\d\s./
Pattern3 = /a*b*c*/
Pattern4 = /a+bc+/
Pattern5 = /ab?/
```

```
D:\Wiley\Codes>ruby Block.rb
Customer Name: Anya
Customer Name: Ken
Customer Name: William
Customer Name: Mark
Customer Name: Steve
Customers are Anya
Customers are Ken
Customers are William
Customers are Mark
Customers are Steve
```

Figure 4.2 The screen output.

Table 4.2 Syntax for Regular Expressions

SYNTAX	WHAT IT STANDS FOR
\d	Matches a digit
\s	Matches white spaces
Period (.)	Matches any character
\w	Matches any character that appears in a general word

Pattern1 is the simplest of all patterns, which consists of the word Perl. You can use this pattern to find Perl in any string. Pattern2 searches for two digits followed by a space, which is followed by any character. For example, 55 D and 36 C both fall into Pattern2. Pattern3, Pattern4, and Pattern5 are a bit different. Notice the three additional symbols shown here, namely, *, +, and ?. The asterisk character searches for zero or more occurrences of a character. Therefore, if you specify a*, then the pattern searches for zero or more occurrences of the letter a. The plus sign searches for one or more occurrences of a character. Therefore, if you have a+, then the pattern would look for one or more occurrences of the letter a. In the same manner, the question mark searches for zero or one occurrence of a character. Table 4.3 lists our explanations.

Table 4.3 Symbols Used in Patterns

SYMBOL	EXPLANATION
*	Zero or more occurrences of the character preceding it
+	One or more occurrences of the character preceding it
?	Zero or one occurrence of the character preceding it

Therefore, Pattern3 searches for zero or more occurrences of a, which is followed by zero or more occurrences of b. This, in turn, is either followed by zero or additional occurrences of c. Pattern4 searches for one or more occurrences of a, which is followed by one occurrence of b, followed by one or more occurrences of c. Pattern5 searches for one occurrence of a, which is followed by zero or one occurrence of b. You have learned to create basic patterns. Now you will learn to use these patterns with conditional statements. The following code will explain this:

```
str = "The exact time is 11:58PM"
expr = /\d\d:\d\d/
if str=~expr
    puts "Pattern found"
else
    puts "Search for some other pattern"
end
```

In this code, you search for a pattern that consists of two digits followed by a colon and then by two digits. To search for the expression in the string str, you use the if statement. To compare a string with an expression, you use the =~ operator. Therefore, you find that to create a regular expression, you only need to enclose the expression within two slashes. Ruby is a pure object-oriented programming language. Therefore, even these expressions should be considered as objects, which is true. Every expression that you create becomes an object of the class Regexp. Therefore, when you write:

```
expr = /\d\d:\d\d/
```

the variable expr becomes an object of the class Regexp. You can check this by calling the method type of the class:

```
puts expr.type
```

This statement will generate the output Regexp.

Because expr is an object, you also can create it using the method new of its class. This becomes another method of creating a regular expression.

Let's view both methods together to understand the code:

```
expr = /\d\d:\d\d/
expr = Regexp.new('\d\d:\d\d')
```

You have learned about the basics of regular expressions. Now you will learn about regular expressions in more detail.

Regular Expressions in Detail

You have learned to use regular expressions. Now, let's see what $ variables are.

$ Variables

Whenever you compare a regular expression with a string and a match is found, Ruby creates a number of variables. Let's discuss these variables one by one. The $& variable contains the matched characters of the string. The $' variable contains all the characters that appear before the match, and $' contains all the characters after the match. The $~ variable also contains the matched characters. In addition, there are nine variables—$1 through $9—that hold parts of the match. Let's learn about the values of these variables by using the following code:

```ruby
str = "The exact time is 11:58PM and it is going to be midnight"
expr = Regexp.new('(\d\d):(\d\d)(..)')
if str=~expr
    puts "Pattern found"
else
    puts "Search for some other pattern"
end
puts "The characters before the match : #{$`}"
puts "The matched characters are: #{$&}"
puts "The characters after the match are: #{$'}"
puts "The matched characters are: #{$~}"
puts "The first part of the match is: #{$1}"
puts "The second part of the match is: #{$2}"
puts "The third part of the match is: #{$3}"
puts $4
puts $5
```

Figure 4.3 shows the output of this code.

```
D:\Wiley\Codes>ruby $_expr.rb
Pattern found
The characters before the match : The exact time is
The matched characters are: 11:58PM
The characters after the match are:  and it is going to be midnight
The matched characters are: 11:58PM
The first part of the match is: 11
The second part of the match is: 58
The third part of the match is: PM
nil
nil
```

Figure 4.3 The output.

As you can see, the first line of output is `Pattern found`, which indicates that the expression is found in the string. Therefore, Ruby creates a number of $ variables. The `$'` variable displays the characters before the match, that is, `The exact time is`. The `$&` variable outputs the matched characters, that is, `11:58pm`. The `$'` variable outputs the characters after the match, that is, `and it is going to be midnight`. The `$~` variable also outputs the matched characters, `11:58pm`. The `$1`, `$2`, and `$3` variables generate the output consisting of the first, second, and third parts of the match, respectively. `$1`, `$2`, and `$3` display `11`, `58`, and `PM`, respectively. The `$4` variable outputs `nil` because there is no fourth part to the match. For the same reason, the output generated by the `$5` through `$9` variables is also `nil`.

You may wonder how exactly these parts are created in matched characters. You can divide an expression into a number of parts by using parentheses. The number of parentheses in the expression becomes equal to the number of parts of the matched characters. Therefore, if you do not have any parentheses, the value of `$1` to `$9` variables will be `nil`.

You have learned about the different variables formed when you match a regular expression with a string. A variable will become populated with values only when the expression or that pattern is found in the string. Otherwise, these variables show the value as `nil`.

Some More Types of Regular Expressions

What if you want to check whether a particular expression occurs at the start or end of a string? In such situations, you use the caret sign (^) and the dollar sign ($). Just precede the expression with the caret sign, and now, when you compare the expression with the string, Ruby checks for the expression at the start of the string. In the same way, when you add a dollar sign at the end of the expression, Ruby checks for the occurrence of the expression at the end of the string. Just as we have the caret and dollar signs, we also have \A, \Z, and \z. \A is similar to the caret sign. It checks for the occurrence of the expression at the start of the string. \Z and \z check for the end of the string. However, if the string terminates with \n, which is a new line character, then \Z ignores the \n character. \Z checks for the occurrence of the expression just before \n. \z always checks for the end of the string, regardless of how the string is terminated. Let's see some examples:

```
expr1 = /\A\d\d/
expr2 = /(.)$/
```

The expr1 expression searches for two digits at the start of the string, and expr2 matches any character at the end of the string. Now how will you search for a period in a string?

There are certain special characters, such as a plus (+), a hyphen (−), an asterisk (*), and a period (.). If you want to find these characters in a string, then you need to precede them with a backslash (\) in your expression. For example, if you want to find out whether a string ends with a period or not, write:

```
expr1 = /\./
```

Just precede the period with a backslash. If you do not include the backslash, then Ruby will match the period with any character. The same applies for all the other special characters.

There also can be one more type of regular expression. In this type, you can specify an expression in square brackets ([ ]). How is this different from other regular expressions that you have seen? When you specify a set of characters in brackets and compare them with the string, Ruby looks for a match with any one of the characters in the brackets. For example:

```
expr1 = [abcde]
```

Ruby will search for one of the characters (a, b, c, d, or e) in the string. The only difference is that in all the previous regular expressions Ruby searches for a pattern of characters in the string, whereas here it searches for only a particular character from the series of characters specified in the brackets. Because the preceding characters a, b, c, d, and e are in sequence, you also can specify the expression as [a-e]. Therefore:

- [A-Z] represents all letters in uppercase.

- [a-z] represents all letters in lowercase.

- [0-9] represents all digits.

In these types of regular expressions, you can use a caret sign (^), but it has a different meaning:

- [^A-Z] stands for all other characters except the uppercase letters. In the same way, you can use the caret sign with lowercase letters and digits.

- [^A-Za-z] stands for no letters, regardless of whether they are in uppercase or lowercase.

This regular expression matches only digits or special characters. You also can specify all the other special characters inside the brackets. Let's consider a code sample:

```
str = "Hello Good Morning!! What is your name?"
expr1=/[!@%^&*(){}:";'?><@*()]/
if str=~expr1
puts "Special character found"
else
puts "Not found"
end
```

The output of this code is:

```
Special character found
```

The special character found is !. You can include all the special characters within brackets.

What if you want to check for two patterns in a string simultaneously? Then you need to specify two patterns separated by a vertical bar (|). Let's see how to use this type of regular expression:

```
str = "Hello Good Morning!! What is your name?"
expr1 = /[!@Z$%^]|abcd/
if str =~ expr1
     puts "Match found"
else
     puts "Match not found"
end
```

Now, in the same expression, you check for two patterns. The two patterns are [!@Z$%^] and abcd. Ruby checks for one of these two patterns in the string str. This vertical bar can be compared with an OR operator. Only when one of the two patterns is found will the condition become true; otherwise, it is false. Because str contains the exclamation point (!), the condition is true, and therefore, the output is Match found.

Object Orientation

Let's now look at the object-oriented part of regular expressions. As you already know, every regular expression is actually an object of the class Regexp. The class Regexp supports a method called match that accepts a string to be matched as the parameter. If the match is successful, then the method returns an object of the class MatchData; otherwise, it returns nil. Then you access the values of all the different $ variables using this MatchData object. Let's examine how this is done:

```
expr1=/(\s*)(a+)(b+)(c+)/
m1=expr1.match("The string is abbcccd")
puts "The data type of m1 is: #{m1.type}"
puts "The matched characters are: #{m1[0]}"
puts "The first part of the match is: #{m1[1]}"
puts "The second part of the match is: #{m1[2]}"
puts "The third part of the match is: #{m1[3]}"
puts "The fourth part of the match is: #{m1[4]}"
puts m1[5]
puts "The characters preceding the match are: #{m1.pre_match}"
puts "The characters after the match are: #{m1.post_match}"
```

Figure 4.4 shows the output of this code.

As you can see from the output, the datatype of m1 is MatchData. Here:

- m1[0] displays the matched characters, abbccc
  - m1.pre_match displays the characters before the match, The string is
  - m1.post_match displays the characters after the match, d
- m1[1] displays the first part of the match,   (space)
- m1[2] displays the second part of the match, a
- m1[3] displays the third part of the match, bb
- m1[4] displays the fourth part of the match, ccc
- m1[5] displays the fifth part of the match, nil

In the same way, m1[6], m1[7], m1[8], and m1[9] will have values of nil.

```
D:\Wiley\Codes>ruby Object_expr.rb
The data type of m1 is: MatchData
The matched characters are:  abbccc
The first part of the match is:
The second part of the match is: a
The third part of the match is: bb
The fourth part of the match is: ccc
nil
The characters preceding the match are: The string is
The characters after the match are: d
```

Figure 4.4 The output.

Table 4.4   Date of Birth Data

CUSTOMER NAME	DATE OF BIRTH
Anya	02/12/1975
Ken	12/25/1973
William	01/01/1970

Problem Statement

Knowledge, Inc., stores information regarding the birthdates of customers in mm/dd/yyyy format. A string picks up these data and displays them. At present, the database contains this information for only three customers. Table 4.4 shows the data.

Strings str1, str2, and str3 pick up the respective information about Anya, Ken, and William. The contents of str1, str2, and str3 are as follows:

```
str1 = "Anya's birthdate is 02-12-1975"
str2 = "Ken's birthdate is 12-25-1973"
str3 = "William's birthdate is 01-01-1970"
```

You need to change the contents of str1, str2, and str3 to display them as follows:

```
str1 = "Anya's birthdate is 12 February 1975"
str2 = "Ken's birthdate is 25 December 1973"
str3 = "William's birthdate is 1 January 1970"
```

Task List

- ✔ **Declare the necessary arrays and the regular expression.**
- ✔ **Write the code to display the output.**
- ✔ **Save and execute the code.**
- ✔ **Verify the output.**

Declare the Necessary Arrays and the Regular Expression

You declare a regular expression that extracts only the date of birth from the string. Then you declare three arrays. One will store the days, the second will store the months, and the third will store the years.

```
str1="Anya's birthdate is 02-12-1975"
str2="Ken's birthdate is 12-25-1973"
str3="William's birthdate is 01-01-1970"
expr1=/(\d\d)-(\d\d)-(\d\d\d\d)/
day = Array.new
month = Array.new
year = Array.new
```

You declare an expression `expr1` that will search for two digits followed by a hyphen. This is followed by two digits, which are followed by a hyphen. Finally, the hyphen is followed by four digits in the three strings `str1`, `str2`, and `str3`.

You declare three arrays. One is `day`, which will store the days of the respective birth dates; the second is `month`, which will store the months; and the third array, `year`, stores the years.

Write the Code to Display the Output

```
if str1=~expr1

        Month[0]=$1
        Day[0]=$2
        Year[0]=$3

end
if str2=~expr1

        Month[1]=$1
        Day[1]=$2
        Year[1]=$3
end
if str3=~expr1

        Month[2]=$1
        Day[2]=$2
        Year[2]=$3
end
```

Whenever a match happens, Ruby creates a number of $ variables. The `$~` variable contains the matched characters. The variables `$1` through `$9` contain parts of the match.

In the first `if` statement, when the match happens, the `$~` variable contains `02-12-1975`. The `$1` variable contains the first part of the match, which is `02`. The `$2` variable contains the second part, which is `12`. The `$3` variable contains the third part, which is `1975`. You store the values of these $ variables in the respective arrays. This implies that the value of the $1 variable is transferred to the Month array. The $2 variable value is transferred to the Day array. The $3 variable value is transferred to the Year array. Note that it is important that you store the values of these $ variables in separate variables, especially when you need to use the match statement more than once. This is due to the fact that whenever the match succeeds between a string and expression, a new set of $ variables is created, and the preceding set is overwritten. There is no way in which you can access the values of the preceding set of $ variables unless you store the variables in separate variables.

With the second if statement, the $~, $1, $2, and $3 variables have the values 12-25-1973, 12, 25, and 1973, respectively. With the third if statement, the $~, $1, $2, and $3 variables have the values 01-01-1970, 01, 01, and 1970, respectively. You store the values of these variables in their respective arrays.

Therefore, the values of the respective arrays are as follows:

- The Month array has the values 02, 12, and 01.

- The Day array has the values 12, 25, and 01.

- The Year array has the values 1975, 1973, and 1970.

Thus we have separated the days, months, and years from the mm/dd/yyyy format. Now, because you have gotten the month numbers, you need to map these numbers to the month names. Let's declare a hash with month numbers as keys and month names as values:

```
hash1={
'01' => "January",
'02' => "February",
'03' => "March",
'04' => "April",
'05' => "May",
'06' => "June",
'07' => "July",
'08' => "August",
'09' => "September",
'10' => "October",
'11' => "November",
'12' => "December"
}
```

As you can see, each month number maps to the month name. The month numbers for which you need to find out the month names are stored in the Month array. Thus we can write:

hash1[Month[0]]. This gives the corresponding name for the month number that is stored as the first element of the Month array.

hash1[Month[1]] and hash1[Month[2]]. This gives the corresponding names for the month numbers stored in the second and third elements of the Month array.

You create a new array, Month names, and store the names of the months in this array:

```
Month_names=Array.new
Month_names[0]=hash1[Month[0]]
Month_names[1]=hash1[Month[1]]
Month_names[2]=hash1[Month[2]]
```

Finally, you need to display the output. You can write:

```
puts "Anya's birthday falls on #{Day[0]} #{Month_names[0]} #{Year[0]}"
puts "Ken's birthday falls on #{Day[1]} #{Month_names[1]} #{Year[1]}"
puts "William's birthday falls on #{Day[2]} #{Month_names[2]}
#{Year[2]}"
```

Save and Execute the Code

Save the code as birthdates.rb, and execute it from the command prompt.

Verify the Output

Verify whether the output is displayed as stated in the problem (Figure 4.5).

```
D:\Wiley\Codes>ruby birthdates.rb
Anya's birthday falls on 12 February 1975
Ken's birthday falls on 25 December 1973
William's birthday falls on 01 January 1970
```

Figure 4.5 The screen output.

Summary

In this chapter you learned that:

- The different control structures are `if..else`, the `while` loop, and the `for` loop.
- There is one more kind of `if` statement, namely, `if..elsif..else`.
- To structure codes, you can use blocks.
- You can access each element of a collection using iterators.
- Each iterator always is associated with a block, whereas with the `collect` iterator, this is not the case.
- You can find a pattern of characters in a string using regular expressions.
- Regular expressions can be created either by specifying the pattern of characters to be found in between the two slashes or by using the object-oriented approach.
- Whenever an expression matches a string, Ruby creates a load of $ variables.

## CHAPTER 5

Methods and Modules

OBJECTIVES

In this chapter you will learn to:

- ✓ Define methods with different types of arguments
- ✓ Pass an array to a method
- ✓ Define modules
- ✓ Implement multiple inheritance using modules

Getting Started

In the preceding chapters you learned to define and implement methods. You learned about two types of methods. One is a simple method, which does not accept any parameter, and the other is a method that accepts one or more parameters. You can represent a simple method like this:

```
def method1
end
```

You can represent a method that accepts parameters like this:

```
def method2 (var1, var2)
end
```

Whenever you call the simple method, you write only the method name, such as:

```
method1
```

However, when you call a method with parameters, you write the method name along with the parameters, such as:

```
method1 25, 35
```

Whatever the type of method, every method performs some type of processing and returns a value. In Ruby, methods always return at least one value. In this chapter you will learn to trap these values.

The most important drawback to using methods with parameters is that you need to remember the number of parameters whenever you call such methods. For example, if a method accepts three parameters and you pass only two, then Ruby displays an error. Therefore, you need to remember the exact number of parameters before calling such methods. In such situations in Ruby you can define a method that accepts any number of parameters. The number of parameters to be passed to the method is not fixed. Such methods are methods that accept variable numbers of parameters. In this chapter, you will learn to declare methods with a variable number of parameters and also learn about methods that allow you to pass an array as a parameter. You also will learn about class methods.

Consider a situation in which you have a group of functions and you want to reuse these functions in some other code. One of the ways to do this is to rewrite the same functions. However, this amounts to a lot of code redundancy. Traditional programming languages such as C and C++ would include the entire group of functions in the new code. Java also does the same thing with the help of the `import` statement. Similar to the `include` statement of C and the `import` statement of Java, you have the `require` statement of Ruby. Using the `require` statement, you can include all the required files whose code you want to reuse. However, using the `require` statement sometimes leads to code ambiguity. The best solution is to use modules. You will learn about modules and how to implement mixins using modules in this chapter.

Methods

You know how to declare a method with arguments. Let us examine how a method is declared with default arguments with the help of this sample code:

```
def test(a1="Ruby", a2="Perl")
     puts "The programming language is #{a1}"
     puts "The programming language is #{a2}"
end
test "C", "C++"
test
```

Figure 5.1 shows the output of this code.

NOTE Method names should begin with a lowercase letter. If you begin a method name with an uppercase letter, Ruby might think that it is a constant and hence can parse the call incorrectly.

In the preceding code, look at the way the method test is declared. The method test takes in two arguments, a1 and a2. In the definition itself, you can see that a1 is assigned the value Ruby, and a2 is assigned the value Perl. This means that whenever the method test is called without parameters, a1 and a2 will have the default values Ruby and Perl, respectively. When parameters are passed, a1 and a2 will take the values of the parameters. Therefore:

```
test "C", "C++"
```

will make the value of a1 become C and the value of a2 become C++. With the statement:

```
test
```

a1 and a2 will have the default values Ruby and Perl.

```
The programming language is C
The programming language is C++
The programming language is Ruby
The programming language is Perl
```

Figure 5.1 The screen output.

Return Values from Methods

Here you will examine how to pass values from methods. As you know, every method in Ruby returns a value by default. Let us declare a method and trap the values it returns. Thus:

```
def test
      i = 100
end
j = test
j = j+1
puts j
```

produces an output of 101.

From this output, you can judge that the method test returns the value i. To capture the value of i, you write:

```
j = test
```

This is a variable followed by the equals operator, which is followed by the call to the function.

What if you declare two or more variables in the method?

```
def test
      i = 100
      j = 10
      k = 0
end
```

This method, when called, will return the last declared variable. The preceding code will return the value of k. What if you want to return the value of i? In this case, you can write:

```
def test
      i = 100
      j = 0
      k = 10
   i
end
```

It is quite simple. You only need to write the name of the variable you want to return at the end of the method. There is one more way to return values from methods. This involves using the return statement followed by the name of the variable.

Therefore, your method becomes:

```
def test
    i = 100
    j = 0
k = 10
    return i
end
```

This code returns the value of the variable i.

You have examined all the different ways to return a value from the method. The question that arises is, Can a method return more than one value? Yes. In Ruby you can return more than one value from a method. Let us see the code to do this:

```
def test
    i = 100
    j = 0
    k = 10
    return i, j, k
end
var = test
puts var
```

The output of this code will be:

```
100
0
10
```

Therefore, when you call the method test by using:

```
var = test
```

the method returns three values for the var variable. Therefore, the var variable becomes an array of three elements. The return statement is the only approach that can return more than one value from a method.

Using a Variable Number of Parameters

Suppose that you declare a method that takes two parameters. Whenever you call this method, you need to pass two parameters along with it.

However, Ruby allows you to declare methods that work with a variable number of parameters. Let us examine a sample of this:

```
def sample (*test)
    puts "The number of parameters is #{test.length}"
    for i in 0...test.length
            puts "The parameters are #{test[i]}"
    end
end
sample "Anya", "25", "F"
```

In this code, you have declared a method `sample` that accepts one parameter `test`. However, this parameter is a variable parameter. This means that this parameter can take in any number of variables. In plain words, you can say that `test` is an array and that the elements of the array `test` will be the parameters that will be passed when you call the method `sample`. You call the method `sample` with values `Anya`, `25`, and `F`. These three values will become the elements of the array `test`. Therefore, the output becomes that shown in Figure 5.2.

In the preceding example, you passed a number of variables as parameters and accepted these variables as a single argument. What has actually happened is that the variables have been converted into the elements of an array. You also can do exactly the opposite. This means that you can pass an array as a parameter whenever you call the method, and in the method, you can accept the array in the form of its individual elements. In short, you will pass one parameter and accept it in different variables. Let us look at some sample code:

```
def sample (a1, a2, a3, a4, a5)
    puts "First element: #{a1}"
    puts "Second element: #{a2}"
    puts "Third element: #{a3}"
    puts "Fourth element: #{a4}"
    puts "Fifth element: #{a5}"
end
array1 = %w(1 2 3 4 5)
sample(*array1)
```

Figure 5.3 shows the output of this code. From the output, you can make out that `array1` that is passed to the method `sample` is broken into individual elements in the method.

```
The number of parameters is 3
The parameters are Anya
The parameters are 25
The parameters are F
```

Figure 5.2   The screen output.

```
First element: 1
Second element: 2
Third element: 3
Fourth element: 4
Fifth element: 5
```

Figure 5.3 The screen output.

Methods and Blocks

You have seen how a block and a method can be associated with each other in Chapter 4. You normally invoke a block by using the `yield` statement from a method that has the same name as that of the block. Therefore, you write:

```
def test
     yield
end
test{ puts "Hello world"}
```

This example is the simplest way to implement a block. You call the test block by using the `yield` statement. In fact, you also can pass a block as a parameter to the method. You will learn how to do this now:

```
def test(&bloc)
     bloc.call
end
test { puts "hello world"}
```

Here you call the method `test` with the block as a parameter. To accept the block, you use a variable preceded by an ampersand (`&`). Then you use the `call` method to invoke the block. Therefore, you can have the statement:

```
bloc. call
```

Class Methods

Whenever you want to access a method of a class, you first need to instantiate the class. Then, using the object, you can access the members of the class. What if you want to access a method without instantiating a class? In such cases, you can use class methods. Let us see how a class method is declared:

```
class Accounts
     def reading_charge
     end
     def Accounts.return_date
     end
end
```

See how the method `return_date` is declared. It is declared with the class name followed by a period, which is followed by the name of the method. You can access this class method directly as follows:

```
Accounts.return_date
```

To access this method, you need not create objects of the class `Accounts`.

Problem Statement

Knowledge, Inc., has two departments, the Library Department and the Accounts Department. Both the departments perform common functions, such as handling resources and performing employee appraisals. Resources are in the form of a number of people and a number of computers. Declare a method `resources` that accepts the number of resources a department has in the form of variable parameters and returns all the values. Display the string `Employee appraisal happens once a year` in the method `employee_appraisal`. Make `employee_appraisal` a class method. Store the name, age, gender details, and invoice total of each customer. In addition, with the help of the block, display the string `The total amount purchased by x is y`. In this string, x represents name of the customer, and y represents total amount. Demonstrate how you will pass a block as a parameter to a method.

Task List

✔ **Declare the class.**

✔ **Declare a method.**

✔ **Create a class.**

✔ **Save and execute the code.**

✔ **Verify the output.**

Declare the Class

Create a class by the name `Department`, and   define the method `resources` with a one-variable parameter. The method `resources` should return all the parameters that are passed to it. Thus:

```
class Department
    def resources(*res)
        @no_of_people=res[0]
        @no_of_comp=res[1]
```

```
                return @no_of_people, @no_of_comp
        end
end
```

You declare a method resources in the class Department. The method resources has a variable parameter, res. This variable will accept two parameters in res[0] and res[1]. The first and second parameters will be stored in the variables @no_of_people and @no_of_comp, respectively. Both the variables will be returned together by using the return statement.

Declare the Method

In the class Department, declare the method employee_appraisal as a class method. You can call this method without creating an object of the class Department. In this method, write the necessary puts statement:

```
def Department.employee_appraisal
            puts "Employee appraisal happens once a year"
end
```

Create a Class

Create a class called Customer with name, age, and gender details and invoice total as its characteristics. Also pass a block as a parameter to the method initialize. Use the block to display the string The total amount purchased by x is y. In this string, x represents name of the customer, and y represents the total amount. Thus:

```
class Customer
     def initialize(name,age,sex,amt,&purchases)
            @name=name
            @age=age
            @sex=sex
            @purchases=purchases
            @amt=amt
            @purchases.call(@amt, @name)

     end
end
Department.employee_appraisal
Dept1=Department.new
y=Dept1.resources(25,10)
puts "Number of people are #{y[0]}"
puts "Number of computers are #{y[1]}"
cust1=Customer.new("Anya",35,"F",2500){|amount, name| puts "The total
```

```
amount purchased by #{name} is #{amount}"}
cust2=Customer.new("Ken",25,"M",1800){|amount, name| puts "The total
amount purchased by #{name} is #{amount}"}
```

You declare a class `Customer` with the method `initialize`. The method accepts the variables `name`, `age`, `sex`, and `amt` as parameters. The method also accepts a block as a parameter in the variable `purchases`. Therefore, the variable `purchases` is preceded by an ampersand (`&`). The values in the variables `name`, `age`, `sex`, `amt`, and `&purchases` are stored in the instance variables `@name`, `@age`, `@sex`, `@amt`, and `@purchases`. Thus the statement:

```
@purchases.call(@amt, @name)
```

calls the block associated with the method `new` of the class `Customer` that has `@amt` and `@name` as parameters:

```
cust1=Customer.new("Anya","35","F","2500"){|amount, name| puts "The
total amount purchased by #{name} is #{amount}"}
```

This statement creates an object `cust1` of the class `Customer`, and the method `new` passes `Anya`, `35`, `F`, and `2500` as parameters:

```
{|amount, name| puts "The total amount purchased by #{name} is
#{amount}"}
```

The previously mentioned block is also passed as a parameter to the method `initialize`:

```
Dept1=Department.new
y=Dept1.resources(25,10)
puts "Number of people are #{y[0]}"
puts "Number of computers are #{y[1]}"
```

`Dept1` becomes the object of the class `Department`. Using `Dept1`, you call the method `resources` with `25` and `10` as parameters. All the values returned by the method `resources` are stored in the variable `y`. The method `resources` returns two values that are stored as `y[0]` and `y[1]` and then are displayed in the `puts` statement.

Save and Execute the Code

Save the code as `Methods.rb`, and execute it from the command prompt.

Verify the Output

Verify whether proper values are displayed by the block (see Figure 5.4).

```
Employee appraisal happens once a year
Number of people are 25
Number of computers are 10
The total amount purchased by Anya is 2500
The total amount purchased by Ken is 1800
```

Figure 5.4   The screen output.

Modules

Modules are similar to classes. Variables, constants, and functions constitute a module. If modules are similar to classes, then why do you need to have two different concepts that implement the same thing? The reason is that according to the object-orientation concept, a class is a broad definition for a particular term. Only if variables and functions together constitute a meaning can you join them together to form a class. What if the variables and functions do not join to yield a proper definition? The answer is that you can still join them together and form a module.

Defining a Module

Let us examine how to define a module:

```
module Week
    First_day = "Sunday"
    def Week.weeks_in_month
            puts "You have four weeks in a month"
    end
    def Week.weeks_in_year
            puts "You have 52 weeks in a year"
    end
end
```

Here, you have a module, Week, with a constant, First_day. Constants always begin with a capital letter. Two methods, weeks_in_month and weeks_in_year, also form part of the module. Like class methods, whenever you define a method in a module, you specify the module name followed by a dot and then the method name. How do you access the data members of the module? There is a difference in the way you access a constant in a module:

```
puts Week::First_day
puts Week.weeks_in_month
puts Week.weeks_in_year
```

To access a constant, you use two colons. You can access a method in a module in the same way that you access class methods.

The `require` **Statement**

The `require` statement is similar to the `include` statement of C and C++ and the `import` statement of Java. All these statements generally are used to avoid rewriting previously written code. Using these statements, you can reuse the existing libraries of programming languages. For example, if you include these two examples in your code, namely:

```
require "Sample.rb"
require "Math.rb"
```

you can access all the functions that are defined in the two files, `Sample.rb` and `Math.rb`. However, what if both the files contain some functions with common names? This will result in code ambiguity. To avoid code ambiguity, you can use modules. This is another advantage of using modules.

Modules and Classes

Can you actually use a module and a class together? The answer is yes. You can embed a module within a class and then use all the existing data members of the module in the class. To embed a module in a class, you use the `include` statement in the class:

```
include modulename
```

Therefore, you can write:

```
class Decade
include Week
     no_of_yrs=10
     def no_of_months
             puts Week::First_day
             number=10*12
             puts number
     end
end
d1=Decade.new
puts Week::First_day
Week.weeks_in_month
Week.weeks_in_year
d1.no_of_months
```

In this way, you can use an entire module within a class.

Mixins

C++ is a programming language that supports multiple inheritance directly. What is multiple inheritance? By now, you know what inheritance is. Inheriting the features of a parent class is inheritance. When a class can inherit features from more than one parent class, the class is supposed to show *multiple inheritance*. Java supports multiple inheritance indirectly by using interfaces. Ruby's answer to multiple inheritance is modules. A module does not provide you with a direct way of implementing multiple inheritance, but it offers you an indirect way. Ruby also terms multiple inheritance a *mixin*. Let us examine the following sample code to gain an understand of mixin:

```ruby
module A
def a1
end
def a2
end
end
module B
    def b1
    end
    def b2
    end
    end
    class Sample
        include A
        include B
        def s1
        end
    end
samp=Sample.new
samp.a1
samp.a2
samp.b1
samp.b2
samp.s1
```

Module A consists of the methods a1 and a2. Module B consists of the methods b1 and b2. The class Sample includes both modules A and B. The class Sample can access all four methods, namely, a1, a2, b1, and b2. Therefore, you can see that the class Sample inherits from both the modules. Thus you can say the class Sample shows multiple inheritance or a *mixin*.

Problem Statement

The Library Department has two sections, Novels and Magazines. Each section is responsible for the maintenance of books related to that section. Each section also maintains a record of the total number of books in the section. You should demonstrate multiple inheritance in the class library from the module Novel and the module Magazine. Novel has a method, no_of_novels, and Magazine has a method, no_of_mag. The Library Department has two functions, maintenance and issuing. The method maintenance should display the string This is the maintenance section of the library, and the method issuing should display the string This is the issuing section of the library. In addition, you should display the number of novels and the number of magazines in the library.

Task List

- ✔ **Declare the modules.**
- ✔ **Declare the class.**
- ✔ **Display the information.**
- ✔ **Save and execute the code.**
- ✔ **Verify the output.**

Declare the Modules

Declare two modules, Novel and Magazine, with no_of_novels and no_of_mag as their methods, respectively. Thus:

```
module Novel
    def no_of_novels
            @no_of_novels=100
            return @no_of_novels
    end
end
module Magazine
    def no_of_mag
            @no_of_mag=350
            return @no_of_mag
    end
end
```

You declared two modules, Novel and Magazine. The Novel module shows the method no_of_novels with @no_of_novels as the instance variable. The Magazine module shows the method no_of_mag with @no_of_mag as the instance variable.

Declare the Class

Declare the class Library with two methods, maintenance and issuing. Display the respective strings in both the methods. Show multiple inheritance in this class from both modules. Thus:

```
class Library
     include Novel
     include Magazine
     def maintenance
            puts "This is the maintenance section of the library"
     end
     def issuing
            puts "This is the issuing section of the library"
     end
end
```

The include statement is used to include a module in a class. Thus:

```
include Novel
include Magazine
```

These statements will include both the modules in the class Library showing multiple inheritance. You also declare two methods, maintenance and issuing, in the class.

Display the Information

Now display the number of novels and the number of magazines in the library:

```
Lib=Library.new
n=lib.no_of_novels
puts "The number of novels is : #{n}"
m=lib.no_of_mag
puts "The number of magazines is : #{m}"
lib.maintenance
lib.issuing
```

You create an object, lib, of the class Library and then call the methods no_of_novels and no_of_mag by using this object. Whatever the methods no_of_novels and no_of_mag return is stored in the variables n and m, respectively.

Save and Execute the Code

Save the code as Module.rb, and execute it from the command prompt.

```
The number of novels is : 100
The number of magazines is : 350
This is the maintenance section of the library
This is the issuing section of the library
```

Figure 5.5 The screen output.

Verify the Output

Verify the values of the number of novels and the number of magazines (see Figure 5.5).

Summary

In this chapter you learned:

- How to return values from methods.
- That you can return one or more values from methods.
- That you can declare a variable number of arguments.
- That you can even pass an array to a method.
- That modules are similar to classes.
- That you can implement a module in a class.
- That you can implement multiple inheritance or mixins by using these modules.

CHAPTER

6

Input and Output

OBJECTIVES

In this chapter you will learn to:

- ✔ **Use input and output statements**
- ✔ **Use the** `File` **and** `IO` **class methods**

Getting Started

Without some way to interact with the outside world, most of our programs would be rather pointless. At the very least, we need to provide input to tell the program what specific set of data we want processed (or what parameters to use in its processing), and we need some way for the program to inform us of the results.

All of Ruby's input-output (I/O) facilities are derived from the class `IO`. The streams we normally expect in programs running under UNIX or Windows are provided as global instances of `IO`: `$stdin`, `$stdout`, and `$stderr`. `$stdin` allows access to the standard input stream. By default, the standard input stream is the keyboard. `$stdout` allows access to the standard output stream. By default, the standard output stream is the screen. $stderr allows access to the standard error stream. By default, the standard error stream is the screen.

The class IO provides all the basic methods, such as read, write, gets, puts, readline, getc, and printf. There are versions of class IO methods available in the top-level execution environment that appear not to be associated with any particular object instance. This seems to violate Ruby's generally object-oriented nature. However, these methods, in fact, are provided by the module Kernel and actually are methods of class Object, which includes Kernel as a mixin. These top-level methods simply call the equivalent methods on an appropriate instance of IO. For example, the top-level gets is actually a call to $stdin.gets, and the top-level puts is a call to $stdout.puts. The remainder of this chapter enumerates all the methods of IO and explains their purposes and uses. The next section discusses some of the statements related to input and output.

Input and Output

gets Statement

In previous chapters, you assigned values to variables and then printed the output. However, in most situations, you will need to do more than just print assigned values. For example, you might need to accept a value from a user and then print the corresponding output based on the user's choice. In such situations, you need to accept values from users. To do so, you use the gets statement. The following code shows you how to use the gets statement. This code will prompt the user to enter a value, which will be stored in a variable val. The puts val statement instructs the program to display the value stored in the variable val. Thus:

```
puts "Enter a value"
val = gets
puts val
```

When you run this code, first the screen will show the following output with the cursor on the next line waiting for an input:

```
Enter a value
```

Whatever the user enters, that value would be stored in the variable val and subsequently displayed on the screen.

putc Statement

Unlike the putc statement, which outputs the entire string onto the screen, the putc statement can be used to output one character at a time. For example, the output of the following code is just the character H:

```
str="Hello"
putc str
```

print Statement

The print statement is similar to the puts statement. The only difference is that the puts statement goes to the next line after printing the contents, whereas with the print statement the cursor is positioned on the same line. Let us examine an example to check out the difference:

```
puts "Hello World"
puts "Good Morning"
```

The output of this code is:

```
Hello World
Good Morning
```

Now let's use the print statement and see what the output will be:

```
print "Hello World"
print "Good Morning"
```

The output of this code is:

```
Hello WorldGood Morning
```

Note the difference in the two outputs. In the first case, puts "Hello World" will display Hello World on the screen. Then the second puts statement, puts "Good Morning", will display Good Morning on the next line. However, using the print statement, the output is not the same. After printing Hello World, the second print statement prints the contents Good Morning on the same line.

The Class File

Until now, you have been reading and writing to the standard input (keyboard) and standard output (monitor) devices. What would you do if you wanted to accept input from a file instead of the keyboard? Other programming languages such as C and C++ have streams to handle such situations. Ruby's answer to streams is the class `File`. The class `File` is the child class of the base class `IO`. The class `IO` handles all the various input and output methods. In this section you will learn about the various methods in the class `File`.

File.new

As the name implies, you can create a new object of the class `File` using the method `new`. The following code snippet illustrates this:

```
file1 = File.new("Sample", "r")
```

This statement creates a new object `file1`. The method `new` takes in two parameters, the name of the file and the mode of the file. The preceding code instructs the program to open the file `sample` in the `read` mode. This file will be assigned to the object `file1`. Once the file is assigned to the object `file1`, you can read from the file using the object `file1`. Other than the `read` mode, there are several other modes in which you can open a file. Table 6.1 lists all the different modes in which you can open a file.

Table 6.1 The Different Modes of Opening a File

MODES	WHAT IT IMPLIES
r	Read-only mode. The file pointer is placed at the beginning of the file. This is the default mode.
r+	Read-write mode. The file pointer will be at the beginning of the file.
w	Write-only mode. Overwrites the file if the file exists. If the file does not exist, creates a new file for writing.
w+	Read-write mode. Overwrites the existing file if the file exists. If the file does not exist, creates a new file for reading and writing.
a	Write-only mode. The file pointer is at the end of the file if the file exists. That is, the file is in the append mode. If the file does not exist, it creates a new file for writing.
a+	Read and write mode. The file pointer is at the end of the file if the file exists. The file opens in the append mode. If the file does not exist, it creates a new file for reading and writing.

Consider the following statement:

```
file1 = File.new("Sample", "r")
```

In this case, you have specified only the file name. This is not enough! You need to specify the full path for the file unless the file is in the current working directory.

Thus the preceding statement should be written as:

```
file1 = File.new("C:\Ruby\Sample", "r")
```

Even this statement will cause problems. The reason is the use of the backslash character (\) while specifying the path. In Ruby, the backslash character has a special meaning. Thus you need to escape this special meaning of backslash. You can do this by using another backslash character. You close the file using the method `close` of the file object.

Thus the correct statement would be:

```
file1 = File.new("C:\\Ruby\\Sample", "r")
file1.close
```

File.open

This method is similar to the `File.new` method. This method can be used to create a new file object and assign that file object to a file. However, there is one difference. The difference is that the `File.open` method can be associated with a block, whereas you cannot do the same using the `File.new` method. Whenever you associate a block with a `File.open` method, the method creates an object and passes it directly to the block. The file gets closed automatically when the block finishes. Let us examine a code snippet to demonstrate the `File.open` method:

```
file2 = File.open("C:\\Ruby\\Sample"){|f| puts "The file object is
#{f}"}
```

The output of this code is:

```
The file object is #<File: 0x459a6d8>
```

The first line of the output displays the ID of the object created. The object ID will differ every time you run the sample code. One more important thing you need to remember is that the `File.open` method creates a file object and passes it directly to the block. You cannot access the file object anywhere outside the block. Thus, if you write a statement such as:

```
puts file2
```

the output shown will be nil.

Sysread

You can use the method sysread to read the contents of a file. You can open the file in any of the modes when using the method sysread. Thus:

```
file3 = File.new("C:\\Ruby\\Sample","r")
file3.sysread(20)
```

This statement will output the first 20 characters of the file. The file pointer will now be placed at the 21st character in the file.

Syswrite

The method syswrite writes the contents of the file. Thus it becomes necessary for the file to be opened in one of the write or append modes. This method writes at the position where the file pointer is placed. Let us look at a snippet of code that illustrates the use of this function:

```
file4 = File.new("C:\\Ruby\\Sample", "r+")
```

This statement will open the file in the read and write mode. The file pointer, by default, will be at the first character. Thus:

```
puts file4.sysread(20)
```

would output the first 20 characters of the file sample. The file pointer would now be at the 21st character position. The statement:

```
file4.syswrite("ABCDEF")
```

will write ABCDEF from the 21st character onward.

each_byte

This method belongs to the class File. The method each_byte is always associated with a block. Consider the following code sample:

```
file5 = File.new("C:\\Ruby\\Sample")
file5.each_byte{|ch| putc ch}
```

Characters are passed one by one to the variable `ch` and then displayed on the screen.

gets

In the preceding section, you used the `gets` statement to accept input from the standard input device, the keyboard. However, to accept input from a file directly, you use the `gets` statement of the class `File`. The following code shows the use of the `gets` statement:

```
file6 = File.new("C:\\Ruby\\Sample")
str=file6.gets
puts str
```

In this code, the `file6.gets` statement will pass the contents of the file `Sample` to the `str` variable. The `puts str` statement will output the contents to the screen.

File Methods

Let us discuss some more methods related to the class `File`. Table 6.2 lists and describes some of the commonly used methods.

IO.readlines

In the preceding section you saw the methods of the class `File`. However, recall that the class `File` is a subclass of the class `IO`. The class `IO` also has some methods that are exclusive to it. Let's now discuss a few methods that

Table 6.2   Methods Related to the Class **File**

METHODS	WHAT IT DOES
atime	Returns the time when the file was last accessed
basename	Returns the name of the file or the directory that appears last in the path
ctime	Returns the time when the file was last changed
dirname	Returns the name of the directory to which the file belongs
ftype	Returns the file type whether it is a file, directory, or socket

are exclusive to the class IO. One of these methods is IO.readlines. This method returns the contents of the file line by line. The following code displays the use of the method IO.readlines:

```
arr = IO.readlines("C:\\Ruby\\Sample")
puts arr[0]
puts arr[1]
```

In this code, the variable arr is an array. Each line of the file Sample will be an element in the array arr. Therefore, arr[0] will contain the first line, whereas arr[1] will contain the second line of the file.

IO.foreach

This method also returns output line by line. The difference between the method foreach and the method readlines is that the method foreach is associated with a block. However, unlike the method readlines, the method foreach does not return an array. Thus this code:

```
IO.foreach("C:\\Ruby\\Sample"){|bloc| puts bloc}
```

will pass the contents of the file Sample line by line to the variable bloc, and then the output will be displayed on the screen.

 ## Problem Statement

Knowledge, Inc. wants customer information such as first name, last name, and email address to be stored in a file. As a programmer on the development team of Knowledge, Inc., Jim is assigned the task of writing code to accept the details from the customer and store those details in the file.

 ## Task List

✔ **Identify the method to be used to create a file object.**
✔ **Write the code to enter details into the file.**
✔ **Save and execute the code.**
✔ **Verify the output.**

Identify the Method to Be Used to Create a File Object

The method File.new is used to create an object of a file. You will store all the details of the customer in a file called customer_details.txt. Let us examine the statement needed to create a file object `fileObj` and assign the file `customer details.txt` to that file object:

```
fileObj = File.new ("C:\\Ruby\\customer_details.txt", "a")
```

In this statement, you have created a file object `fileObj` and assigned it to the file `customer_details.txt` that is in the folder `C:\Ruby`. You have opened the file in the append mode.

Write the Code to Enter Details into the File

First, you will accept the details such as first name, last name, and email address from the customer and then store them into the `customer details.txt` file. Thus:

```
puts "Enter your first name"
first_name=gets
puts "Enter your last name"
last_name=gets
puts "Enter your email address"
email=gets
```

This code accepts the details first name, last name, and email address and stores them in the variables `first_name`, `last_name`, and `email`, respectively. Then you need to store all these details into an array. Let us first define an array:

```
customer_info=[]
```

This will create the array `customer info`. At present, it is empty.

Now you add the values of these variables as elements of the array `customer_info`:

```
customer_info[0]=first_name
customer_info[1]=last_name
customer_info[2]=email
```

There is another method of adding elements to an array. Let us examine it:

```
customer_info.push(first_name)
customer_info.push(last_name)
customer_info.push(email)
```

The method `push` is a method of class `Array`. Thus you can call the method and pass the value as a parameter to that method. Once you have stored all the values into an array, then you will use the method `syswrite` to write the array contents into the file `customer_details.txt`. The statement:

```
fileObj.syswrite(customer_info)
```

will store the contents of the array   `customer_info` into the file `customer_details.txt`.

Save and Execute the Code

Save the code as `customer_info.rb`, and execute it from the command prompt.

Verify the Output

You can verify whether all the customer details have been entered properly into the file by reading the contents of the file. You can read the contents of the file by using the method `IO.foreach`. Let us examine how to use the method `IO.foreach`:

```
puts "The contents of the file are as follows:"
IO.foreach("C:\\Ruby\\customer_details.txt"){|Info| puts Info}
```

The method `IO.foreach` will output the contents of the file `customer_details.txt` line by line to the variable `Info` in the block. Then the `puts Info` statement will output the contents to the screen.

Thus, if the customer enters these values:

```
First name: John
Last name: Doe
Email address: johndoe@serviceprovider.com
```

then the output will be as shown in Figure 6.1.

```
Enter your first name
Jonathan
Enter your last name
Greene
Enter your email address
jgreene@ivmail.com
```

Figure 6.1   Output when the given values are entered.

Summary

In this chapter you learned that:

- The class `Object` is the base class of all the classes in Ruby.
- The class `Object` includes the module `Kernel` that contains various methods related to input and output such as `puts`, `putc`, `gets`, and `readline`.
- The class `File` is a subclass of the base class `IO`.
- The class `File` also consists of various methods related to the file such as `File.new`, `File.open`, `sysread`, and `syswrite`.

Exceptions

Getting Started

In any program there are occasions when things go wrong. People enter invalid data, files you expect to exist are not there (or you do not have permission to access them), memory runs out, a programmer using your library module passes the wrong parameters to one of your methods, and so on. There are a number of ways to handle these sorts of issues. The simplest idea is to just exit the program when anything goes wrong in the method.

A less-drastic approach is to have every method return some kind of status information to say whether its processing was successful and then to test those return values all the way through your code. This can lead to quite messy code where the tests deviate from the main processing performed by the program.

An alternative, which is currently in favor, is to use `exceptions`. When something goes wrong (in other words, an *exceptional* condition occurs), an `exception` is raised to indicate that something unexpected has happened. At some higher level in the program there will be a piece of code that watches for the appearance of that signal and handles it as is deemed appropriate.

There also may be many exception handlers in a given program. Each handler specifies what types of exceptions it knows how to process. An `exception` percolates up until it encounters the first handler that can handle that particular type. If no such handler exists, the `exception` eventually will reach the topmost level, and the program will terminate. This is the approach taken by C++, Java, and Ruby.

Handling Exceptions

Imagine a program such as a text editor. The user needs to enter a name into a Save As dialog and press the OK button. Because the user can specify an arbitrary place to put the file, it is possible that he or she does not have permission to write there. How do we handle this situation?

We could try to work out whether writing to the file will succeed by checking the user's level of access and only attempting to write the file if the user has permission. However, file access problems are not the only issue. If the file system is almost full, we could run out of space in the middle of writing the file. Maybe the place the user wants to store the file in is on a file server, and the network could go down in the middle. As you may have gathered, trying to determine in advance that our action will succeed is almost inevitably doomed to failure.

So how can we handle all the things that can go wrong, even things we have not thought of? The answer is, of course, to use exceptions! Consider the following code:

```
precious = create_masterpiece()
location = ask_user()
begin
  File.open(location, "w") do |file|
  save_work(file, precious)
```

```
end
rescue
  puts "Your save failed. The problem was #{$!}."
end
```

Now, if something goes wrong, either when opening the file for writing or in the middle of saving the data to it, the programmer will be notified. Rather than our program terminating and the user losing his or her work, he or she gets a second chance.

Everything from begin to rescue is protected. If an exception occurs during the execution of this block of code, control is passed to the block between rescue and end.

In this case, we have not indicated what kinds of exceptions we want to catch because we do not really know all the things that could go wrong. You will see how to be more specific in the following section. Notice the global variable $! we used in our error message. This contains the exception that was raised, allowing us to look at what has happened so that we can customize our handling appropriately.

To handle only certain types of exceptions, we specify them as part of the rescue statement. For example, if all we want to handle are errors that occur while writing a file to a disk, we could use the following statement:

```
rescue IOError
```

To specify more than one type, a comma-separated list can be specified:

```
rescue IOError, SystemCallError
```

If we are handling more than one type like this, we may want to know which error occurred. We can use the type field of $! to determine what happened:

```
rescue IOError, SystemCallError
  if $!.type == IOError
    $stderr.puts "A write to the disk failed -- $!."
  else
    $stderr.puts "There was a system call failure -- $!."
  end
end
```

We can safely assume that if the exception is not an IOError, then it must be a SystemCallError because it is guaranteed that the only exceptions of the type specified in the rescue statement will end up in this block of code. Any others either will have been handled further down or will percolate further up.

Ruby makes this simpler. We can provide separate blocks of code for each type of exception:

```
rescue IOError
  puts "A write to the disk failed -- $!."
rescue SystemCallError
  puts "There was some a system call failure -- $!."
end
```

We also can make the code a little more readable by placing the raised exception into a named variable to avoid having to use $!:

```
rescue IOError => io_error
  puts "A write to the disk failed -- #{io_error}."
rescue SystemCallError => system_error
  puts "There was some a system call failure -- #{system_error}."
end
```

What happens if there is another rescue statement somewhere further down in the block of code we are protecting that also mentions one of these exception types or that catches all types? Wait, this sounds a little strange. Why would a rescue block catch an exception if it was not capable of handling it? One good reason would be that the lower level has more information as to what was happening at the time of the exception.

For example, if an IOError occurred, the lower-level code would know precisely how far we had progressed in writing the data out when the exception occurred. It therefore could output a more precise error message and then reraise the exception so that our rescue block could catch it and do whatever general processing we wish to, such as giving the user a second chance to save the file.

Note that when we write rescue SomeError, what we are saying is that we are willing to handle an exception of type SomeError or any type that is derived from it. Therefore, if handling is to be done at different levels in the code, the handler for a base class should be at a higher level than that of any derived classes. If not, then the handlers for the derived classes are redundant, unless the base class handler reraises the exceptions.

One final point about exception handlers: Sometimes it may be possible to recover from an error condition. Consider our Save As example again. If we could determine that the reason an IOError was raised was that the file system is full, then it might be possible to make more space available by deleting some temporary files. Once we have done so, it would make sense to make another attempt to save the data.

Ruby provides a `retry` command to achieve this, as in the following example:

```
precious = create_masterpiece()
location = ask_user()
begin
  File.open(location, "w") do |file|
    save_work(file, precious)
end
rescue IOError => io_error
  puts "I/O error #{io_error}; attempting to make space."
  remove_temp_files()
  retry
rescue SystemCallError => system_error
  puts "A system call failed -- #{system_error}."
end
```

Class Exception

Ruby's standard classes and modules raise exceptions. All the exception classes form a hierarchy, with the class `Exception` at the top. The next level contains seven different types:

- `Interrupt`
- `NoMemoryError`
- `SignalException`
- `ScriptError`
- `StandardError`
- `SystemExit`

No, you haven't miscounted. There is one other exception at this level, `Fatal`, but the Ruby interpreter only uses this internally.

Both `ScriptError` and `StandardError` have a number of subclasses, but we do not need to go into the details here. The important thing is that if we create our own exception classes, they need to be subclasses of either class `Exception` or one of its descendants. Let's look at an example:

```
class FileSaveError < StandardError
  attr_reader :reason
  def initialize(reason)
```

```
    @reason = reason
  end
end
```

We'll look in detail at how exceptions are raised in the next section, but for now let's just look at one example:

```
File.open(path, "w") do |file|
  begin
  # Write out the data ...
  rescue
  # Something went wrong!
    raise FileSaveError.new($!)
  end
end
```

The important line here is `raise FileSaveError.new($!)`. We call `raise` to signal that an exception has occurred, passing it a new instance of `FileSaveError`, with the reason being that specific exception caused the writing of the data to fail.

Raising Exceptions

We saw in the preceding section that we could raise a specific exception by constructing an instance of an object derived from the class `Exception`. There are two other ways to raise an exception. First, if the argument to `raise` is a string, then an exception of type `RunTimeError` is automatically constructed and raised. For example:

```
raise "An error has occurred"
```

We discussed the final form, in passing, when we mentioned that handlers for base exception classes normally should be at a higher level in the code than their descendants. We then said that sometimes we wish to partially handle an exception at one level of the code, where we have more specific information about the problem, but then reraise it so that further processing can be performed higher up. If we wish to raise the same exception that we are currently handling, we just need to issue a `raise` with no parameters.

Catch and Throw

Sometimes we will find ourselves in a deeply nested piece of code only to discover that, for some reason, we either no longer can or no longer need to continue with the current processing. An example might be when we are reading a complex data structure and find an error in the data that means we know that the overall structure is invalid. We can handle this kind of situation by using `throw` and `catch`. This is similar to how normal exceptions are raised and handled.

A `catch` block is defined by specifying a symbol that serves as a label, as in the following example, which is a mock-up of a parser for Hypertext Markup Language (HTML) tables:

```
line = gets
catch :syntaxError do
  if line =~ /<table>/
    while (line = gets) !~ /<\/table>/
      if line =~ /<tr>/
        while (line = gets) !~ /<\/tr>/
          if line =~ /<td>/
            # Process this table data item
          else
            # We didn't find the expected
            # <td> tag ...
throw :syntaxError
          end
        end
      end
    end
  end
end
```

At the point where the `throw :syntaxError` occurs, we are nested four levels deep. We potentially could recover from the syntax error by setting a flag and testing it at every level. However, that is very messy. When the `throw` is processed, the Ruby interpreter transfers control to the end of the `catch` block with the corresponding label.

Note that it is not necessary for the `throw` to be nested within the `catch` block. It simply needs to be somewhere in the scope containing the `catch`.

Problem Statement

As a programmer on the development team of Knowledge, Inc., Jim was assigned the task of writing code to accept details such as first name, last name, and email address from customers and store those details into a file. Jim, not being experienced in Ruby, has come up with elementary code that accepts customer details only once. Moreover, Jim has not provided any solution in the code that can take care of unknown errors generated by the code. Mike, being the technical lead in this project, has decided to take Jim off this project and replace him with Adam. Adam has now been given the responsibility of making the code handle more customers and also implement exceptions in the code. Mike also wants Adam to test the code for exceptions.

Task List

- ✓ **Identify the necessary changes to be made to Jim's code.**
- ✓ **Write the code to implement the necessary changes.**
- ✓ **Save and execute the code.**
- ✓ **Test the code for exceptions.**

Identify the Necessary Changes to Be Made to Jim's Code

The code written by Jim is as follows:

```
fileObj = File.new ("C:\\customer_details.txt", "a")
puts "Enter your first name"
first_name=gets
puts "Enter your last name"
last_name=gets
puts "Enter your email address"
email=gets
customer_info=[]
customer_info[0]=first_name
customer_info[1]=last_name
customer_info[2]=email
fileObj.syswrite(customer_info)
```

According to Adam, Jim has implemented the methods of the class `File` and the method `gets` correctly. To make this code robust, Adam has decided to implement a control structure to handle the details of multiple customers. The control structure he has decided to use is the `while` loop. To implement exceptions, Adam will use the `begin..rescue..end` statements to ensure that the code does not throw an unknown error while opening the file.

Write the Code to Implement the Necessary Changes

Adam has decided to implement the `while` loop part first:

```
fileObj = File.new ("C:\\customer_details.txt", "a")
puts "Do you want to enter your details"
puts "Enter 1 for Yes and 0 for No"
choice=gets
choice=choice.to_i
while (choice == 1)
puts "Enter your first name"
first_name=gets
puts "Enter your last name"
last_name=gets
puts "Enter your email address"
email=gets
customer_info=[]
customer_info[0]=first_name
customer_info[1]=last_name
customer_info[2]=email
fileObj.syswrite(customer_info)
puts "Do you want to enter again"
puts "Enter 1 for Yes and 0 for No"
choice=gets
choice=choice.to_i
end
```

The `gets` method accepts all values in the form of characters. Thus you convert the character to an integer using the method `to_i`. Therefore, first the `choice` variable contains the number 1 or 0 in the form of a character. Then `choice=choice.to_i` will convert the value of the `choice` variable to an integer.

The next part is opening the file and reading the contents. Here Adam has decided to implement exceptions because opening a file can generate an error such as `File not found`. Let us look at the code:

```
begin
names=IO.readlines("C:\\customer_details.txt")
count=names.length
for i in 0...count
    puts "The contents of the file are #{names[i]}"
end
rescue
    $stderr.puts "You are in for trouble from Mike"
    puts "The error occurred is #{$!}"
end
```

If the method IO.readlines is not able to find the file customer_details.txt in the C drive, control would be transferred directly to the rescue statement, and the statements between the rescue and end keywords will be executed.

Save and Execute the Code

Save the code as Exceptions.rb, and execute the code from command prompt.

Test the Code for Exceptions

To test the code, Mike wants Adam to enter any fictitious file name and check to see whether the statements between the rescue and end keywords are executed. Adam enters a file name as customer_details1. txt and checks the code. The code now becomes:

```
begin
names=IO.readlines("C:\\customer_details1.txt")
count=names.length
for i in 0...count
     puts "The contents of the file are #{names[i]}"
end
rescue
     $stderr.puts "You are in for trouble from Mike"
     puts "The error occurred is #{$!}"
end
```

You will enter details of two customers when asked for by the code. The details are:

```
First name: Jonathan
Last name: Greene
Email address: jgreene@ivmail.com
First name: Jim
Last name: Anderson
Email address: Json@homework.com
```

Figure 7.1 shows the code output when the given details for customers are entered. The figure also shows the implementation of exceptions.

```
Do you want to enter your details
Enter 1 for Yes and 0 for No
1
Enter your first name
Jonathan
Enter your last name
Greene
Enter you email address
jgreene@ivmail.com
Do you want to enter again
Enter 1 for Yes and 0 for No
1
Enter your first name
Jim
Enter your last name
Anderson
Enter your email address
Json@homework.com
Do you want to enter again
Enter 1 for Yes and 0 for No
0
You are in for trouble from Mike
The error occurred is No such file or directory - "C:\\customer_details2.txt"
```

Figure 7.1 The code output.

Summary

In this chapter, you learned that:

- Exceptions are used to handle unknown errors thrown by a program.

- The code that might throw an error needs to be written between the two keywords begin and rescue, and the code that will handle that unknown error needs to be written between rescue and end.

- The global variable $! will give the type of error that has occurred.

- IOError is the error that is generated during an input or output operation.

- SystemCallError is the error that defines other system errors.

- There are seven exception classes derived from the class Exception, and they are Interrupt, NoMemoryError, SignalException, ScriptError, StandardError, SystemExit, and Fatal.

- You can raise your own custom exceptions by using the keyword raise.

- The catch and throw blocks can be used to handle complex data structures.

CHAPTER

8

Multithreading

OBJECTIVES

In this chapter you will learn to:

- ✔ **Create threads**
- ✔ **Manipulate threads**
- ✔ **Use the class** `Mutex`
- ✔ **Schedule threads**
- ✔ **Discuss multiprocessing**

Getting Started

Many programs are designed to do just one thing at a time. However, situations often occur where some processing logically could be set aside if we had the facility to do so. For example, it would be very annoying if your mail application did not allow you to read any of your mail while it was talking to your Internet connection either because it was downloading new mail or because it was sending the last message you posted. Similarly, imagine if a Web server could interact with only a single user at a time. Considering how many people want to access some Web sites, you could be waiting a very long time to make it to the front of the queue!

As a final example, consider a word processor. When you decide to print your document, it would be really painful if you were forced to wait for the current version to print out before you could continue working on it, particularly if there were other documents queued up at the printer. Fortunately, Web servers, mail applications, and word processors are designed so that they do a number of things at the same time. Two of the most common methods used to achieve this are multithreading and multiprocessing. Ruby provides both these features.

Each of these techniques involves splitting a problem into a number of pieces and allowing them to run more or less in parallel (obviously, they cannot truly run at the same time unless you have more than one central processing unit, or CPU). The essential difference is that in multithreading the pieces are parts of the same program, whereas in multiprocessing, some of the tasks are handled by other programs.

For most of this chapter we will discuss multithreading. The last part of this chapter discusses multiprocessing. The primary advantage of creating multithreaded applications is that you can write efficient programs that will make maximum use of the CPU by keeping idle time to a minimum. Before getting down to designing multithreaded applications, let us first understand the difference between a single-threaded and a multithreaded application.

Single-Threaded Applications

Applications that have only one thread are called *single-threaded applications*. This thread is the main thread of the application. In these applications, all the processing is done in a linear fashion. In other words, the same thread handles user inputs, as well any processing that does not require user input. If that application is waiting for a user input, it cannot perform any background task during that time because there is only one thread. Therefore, single-threaded applications and the operation on which it is running are not able to effectively switch between various independent tasks. Such applications also take a longer time to execute.

Let's try to comprehend this explanation better with the help of an example, `SingleThread.rb`, that uses a single-threaded application. This program contains two functions and executes them one after the other:

```
def func1
    i=0
    while i<=3
    puts "func1 at: #{Time.now}"
    sleep(2)
    i=i+1
    end
end
def func2
    j=0
    while j<=3
    puts "func2 at: #{Time.now}"
    sleep(1)
    j=j+1
    end
end
puts "Started At #{Time.now}"
func1()
func2()
puts "End at #{Time.now}"
```

In this code we have created two methods, func1() and func2(). We also have used the method sleep() in these two methods. The method sleep() takes any value as an argument and halts the execution for those many number of seconds. The body of func1() contains a call to the method sleep() with an argument of 2 seconds. Similarly, func2() contains a call to the method sleep() with an argument of 1 second. This means that whenever the program execution encounters these method calls, the program execution will be halted for specified number of seconds. Because func1() and func2() are called sequentially, the execution of func1() completes first before func2() starts to execute. We have used Time.now to indicate the current system time. The total program execution takes 13 seconds. The output of execution of SingleThread.rb is as shown in the Figure 8.1:

```
Started At Mon Jan 14 12:27:16 GMT+5:30 2002
func1 at: Mon Jan 14 12:27:16 GMT+5:30 2002
func1 at: Mon Jan 14 12:27:18 GMT+5:30 2002
func1 at: Mon Jan 14 12:27:20 GMT+5:30 2002
func1 at: Mon Jan 14 12:27:22 GMT+5:30 2002
func2 at: Mon Jan 14 12:27:24 GMT+5:30 2002
func2 at: Mon Jan 14 12:27:26 GMT+5:30 2002
func2 at: Mon Jan 14 12:27:26 GMT+5:30 2002
func2 at: Mon Jan 14 12:27:27 GMT+5:30 2002
End at Mon Jan 14 12:27:28 GMT+5:30 2002
```

Figure 8.1 Output of SingleThread.rb after execution.

Multithreaded Applications in Ruby

Let's see how much time is taken to execute the same program using multithreading in Ruby:

```
def func1
    i=0
    while i<=3
    puts "func1 at: #{Time.now}"
    sleep(2)
    i=i+1
    end
end
def func2
    j=0
    while j<=3
    puts "func2 at: #{Time.now}"
    sleep(1)
    j=j+1
    end
end
puts "Started At #{Time.now}"
t1=Thread.new{func1()}
t2=Thread.new{func2()}
t1.join
t2.join
puts "End at #{Time.now}"
```

Here, most of the code remains the same as the single-threaded application code. We have created two threads, t1 and t2. The t1 thread executes the method func1. The t2 thread executes the method func2. The beauty of threading is that when one thread sleeps, the other thread takes over the CPU, and when this thread goes to sleep, some other thread takes over the CPU. Therefore, CPU idle time is kept to a minimum. The preceding code involves creating threads and joining threads. We will learn about these two concepts in the next section. At present, you will just execute the code (Figure 8.2). You will notice that the time taken to execute the code is only 9 seconds, whereas it took 13 seconds with single-threaded application.

```
Started At Mon Jan 14 12:29:12 GMT+5:30 2002
func1 at: Mon Jan 14 12:29:12 GMT+5:30 2002
func2 at: Mon Jan 14 12:29:12 GMT+5:30 2002
func2 at: Mon Jan 14 12:29:13 GMT+5:30 2002
func1 at: Mon Jan 14 12:29:14 GMT+5:30 2002
func2 at: Mon Jan 14 12:29:14 GMT+5:30 2002
func2 at: Mon Jan 14 12:29:15 GMT+5:30 2002
func1 at: Mon Jan 14 12:29:16 GMT+5:30 2002
func1 at: Mon Jan 14 12:29:18 GMT+5:30 2002
End at Mon Jan 14 12:29:20 GMT+5:30 2002
```

Figure 8.2   Output of MultiThread.rb after execution.

NOTE The system date and time would change depending on when the code is executed.

Creating a Web Server

Problem Statement

The development team of Knowledge, Inc., has been asked to create a Web server by using Ruby. So the team is planning to use the concept of threading to create the Web server. Because the team is very new and does not have much experience with Ruby, the members have decided to implement a sample Web server that would just show the current date and time when accessed from the client machine. Mike, being the most experienced in using Ruby, is the technical lead for this project. Mike has instructed the development team to implement the concept of mutual exclusion and thread scheduler.

Task List

✔ **Identify the different classes to be used.**
✔ **Implement the Web page.**
✔ **Complete the processing of all the current requests before shutting down the Web server.**
✔ **Implement the class** `Mutex`**.**
✔ **Implement the thread scheduler.**
✔ **Save and execute the code.**
✔ **Verify the output.**

Identify the Different Classes to Be Used

Let's look at how you can code the Web server mentioned in the case study. You might have a class called `RequestHandler` that processes a single request from someone's browser. Without some kind of parallel execution, you would have only one `RequestHandler` instance at any given time, and all other requests would have to queue up, waiting for our program to finish processing the current request. However, using multithreading, you can improve the overall response time by creating a new `RequestHandler` instance each time a request is received and allowing that instance to run on its own thread.

Before you look at some code, you need to discuss how one might organize to receive the requests. Ruby provides a standard class called TCPServer that hides all the complex details of the operating system processes.

You simply need to specify on what IP address and port number you are willing to accept those connections. In this case, you can specify 0.0.0.0 as the address because we are happy to accept any connections that make it to our machine and port number 8888. The standard port number for Hypertext Transfer Protocol (HTTP), the underlying protocol that Web traffic uses, is 80, so hopefully using 8888 will not interfere with any real server that is running on our machine. Let's see how you could write your multithreaded Web server:

```
require 'thread'
require 'socket'
class RequestHandler
def initialize(session)
@session = session
end
def process
# Here, you will be adding all the details of responding to requests
end
end
server = TCPServer.new("0.0.0.0", "8888")
while (session = server.accept)
Thread.new(session) do |newSession|
RequestHandler.new(newSession).process
end
end
```

Implement the Web Page

As you can see, it did not take much work to make things multithreaded. All you did was construct an instance of class Thread and pass it a block of code to execute. Each time a connection comes in from a Web browser, server.accept will return a TCPSocket object that is connected to the browser. You simply pass this to the RequestHandler object when you create it and then ask it to process the request.

To help you to try out an implementation of a Web server, here is a simple implementation of RequestHandler#process that always returns a Web page containing the current time. Do not worry if you cannot understand the details—just give it a try.

```
def process
while @session.gets.chop.length != 0
end
# Send the current time as our response. First
# the headers to tell the browser that this is
# an HTTP response and that the content we are
# sending is HTML
@session.puts "HTTP/1.1 200 OK"
@session.puts "content-type: text/html"
@session.puts "" # End of headers
# Now, the HTML for your page (Time.now is the
# current time) ...
@session.puts "<html>"
@session.puts "  <body>"
@session.puts "    <center>"
@session.puts "      <b>#{Time.now}</b>"
@session.puts "    <center>"
@session.puts "  </body>"
@session.puts "</html>"
# Finally, close the connection, so the browser
# will know the response is finished ...
@session.close
end
```

Try running the complete program and then accessing it from your favorite Web browser using the URL http://localhost: 8888.

You might be wondering what data a thread's code can access. Each thread has its own namespace, so any variables you create in its block of code, including in other methods it calls, are local to that thread. This means that threads cannot change each other's data by mistake.

In addition to its own data, a thread can access any variables that were in existence at the time the thread was created. Why didn't we make use of this in our case study? Why do we have a block local variable newSession that is just a copy of session?

Once the thread has been created, it will effectively run in parallel with the main code and with any other threads that have been created for previous requests but have not yet completed. If you had simply used session instead of creating a copy of it, any new request received could overwrite session before you finished creating the RequestHandler instance.

Thus you potentially could end up with a new handler connected to the next browser that made a request rather than the one you intended. The result would be that one of the requests would receive no response, and the other would be sent two pages, with all the HTML code jumbled up together!

In contrast, `newSession` is local to the thread and hence will not be modified when `session` changes. Thus you can use it safely to construct the new handler.

Complete Processing of All the Current Requests Before Shutting Down the Web Server

A Web server is intended to be running continuously. However, some programs are designed to execute for some period of time and then exit. For example, the user normally will leave a word processor once he or she has finished working on a document.

Normally, when the main thread of a program finishes, the Ruby interpreter will exit, killing any other threads that are still running. This obviously would be a problem if, say, a word processor were still in the middle of sending a document to the printer when the user decided to shut it down.

To avoid this type of problem, rather than simply exiting, a thread can be suspended until another thread has completed. This is done using `Thread#join`. For example, you could change your Web server so that it can be shut down gracefully, making sure that the processing of any current requests is finished before you exit:

```
server = TCPServer.new("0.0.0.0", "8888")
$currentRequests = []
$requestedToShutDown = false
while !$requestedToShutDown
session = server.accept
thread = Thread.new(session) do |newSession|
RequestHandler.new(newSession).process
end
$currentRequests.push(thread)
end
$currentRequests.each { |t| Thread.join(t) }
```

In this case, the Web server accepts requests until the global flag `$requestedToShutDown` is set. This might be done, for example, as part of `RequestHandler`'s processing of some predefined request.

Once the flag is set, the Web server drops out of its main loop. It then runs through all the current handler threads, joining each in turn. By the time all these joins complete, all requests will have been processed, so you can exit safely.

Implement the Mutex Class

If you look at the code a little more closely, you will see that there is a bit of a problem. Because the Web server normally will run for a very long time, during which it will process potentially hundreds of thousands of requests, our $currentRequests array is going to become rather large.

Obviously, all you can do is have each thread remove its own entry from the array once it finishes handling the request it was assigned to process. In theory, this is fairly easy to do because the class Array has a method delete, so this can be coded as:

```
$currentThreads.delete(Thread.current)
```

Here, Thread.current returns the instance that is currently running, which is what you want.

However, remember that all threads have access to this global variable and they are running in parallel. Therefore, it is possible that while one thread is in the middle of removing its entry from the array, another thread could attempt to do the same thing, or the main thread could attempt to add a new handler. In either case, this potentially could leave the array's contents scrambled.

This is a well-known issue in areas such as operating systems and language interpreters that provide this kind of parallel processing. What you require is *mutual exclusion*; in other words, you want only one thread to be accessing the shared variable at a time.

Ruby provides the class Mutex to handle this situation. Here is how you would recode using a Mutex:

```
server = TCPServer.new("0.0.0.0", "8888")
$currentRequests = []
$requestedToShutDown = false
$mutex = Mutex.new
while !$requestedToShutDown
session = server.accept
thread = Thread.new(session) do |newSession|
RequestHandler.new(newSession).process
$mutex.synchronize do
$currentRequests.delete(Thread.current)
end
end
$mutex.synchronize { $currentRequests.push(thread) }
end
$currentRequests.each { |t| Thread.join(t) }
```

The Ruby interpreter guarantees that only one thread will ever be allowed to execute inside a block passed to Mutex#synchronize. If any other thread attempts to enter such a block, it will be queued until the current thread leaves its synchronized block.

Implement the Thread Scheduler

Sadly, there is still a problem here. If you happen to be very unlucky, the new request might be handled before the main thread has a chance to add its handler thread into the array. In this case, the delete method would fail. How can you avoid this?

The Ruby interpreter contains a component called the *thread scheduler* that provides facilities to allow us some control over how the threads in our program execute. To solve your current problem, what you can do is make sure that the new thread you have created does not begin executing until you have a chance to push it into the array. You can achieve this by telling the scheduler that the main thread is in a critical piece of processing that should not be interrupted:

```
session = server.accept
Thread.critical = true
thread = Thread.new(session) do |newSession|
RequestHandler.new(newSession).process
$mutex.synchronize do
$currentRequests.delete(Thread.current)
end
end
$mutex.synchronize { $currentRequests.push(thread) }
Thread.critical = false
```

Thread Priority

Another thing that is sometimes useful is the ability to give threads different processing times. The scheduler also allows you to do this. All you need to do is to set the thread's priority variable. For example:

```
$slow = 0
$fast = 0
(Thread.new { loop { $slow += 1 } }).priority = -2
(Thread.new { loop { $fast += 1 } }).priority = -1
sleep 1
Thread.critical = true
puts "The slow thread counted to #{$slow}"
puts "The fast thread counted to #{$fast}"
```

Here you have given the slow thread a priority lower than the fast one. Notice, by the way, how you have stopped the two threads after the main thread finishes sleeping by again setting Thread.critical. On execution, this code produces:

```
The slow thread counted to 11675
The fast thread counted to 629474
```

NOTE This output can differ from computer to computer.

As you can see, a small difference in priority can make a big difference when the code contains a tight loop like this. Additional features of the scheduler are the ability to start and stop threads.

A given thread can suspend its own execution by calling Thread.stop or explicitly give control back to the scheduler to allow it to start a different thread by calling Thread.pass. One thread can allow another specific thread to run by calling Thread.run.

Here is a simple example of the use of Thread.stop, Thread.pass, and Thread.run:

```
# Threads A and B both loop continually, printing one message,
# sleeping for half a second, and then passing control to another
# thread
threadA = Thread.new do
i = 0
loop do
puts "Thread A: #{i += 1}"
sleep 0.5
Thread.pass
end
end
threadB = Thread.new do
i = 0
loop do
puts "Thread B: #{i += 1}"
sleep 0.5
Thread.pass
end
end
# Thread C also loops continually, printing a message. However,
# it stops after each message, waiting to be woken up again by
# another thread (in this case, the main program)
threadC = Thread.new do
i = 0
loop do
puts "Thread C: #{i += 1}"
```

```
Thread.stop
end
end
# The main program loops continually, doing nothing other than
# sleeping for half a second and then letting Thread C have a
# go
loop do
sleep 0.5
threadC.run
end
```

One last thing: Just as `Thread.join` suspends the current thread until a specific thread exits, `Thread.value` suspends it until the thread's block returns a value.

Save and Execute the Code

Save the code as `WebServer.rb`, and run the code from the command prompt.

Verify the Output

1. Open any browser.
2. On the address bar, type `http://localhost:8888`.
3. Compare the output of the browser with Figure 8.3. You also can check the output from the other client computers. If you are testing on any other client computer, then on the address bar you need to type `http://computer name:8888`, where `computer name` is the name of the computer on which the Web server code is running.

In addition to the preceding concepts, you need to learn one more important concept—multiprocessing. We discuss multiprocessing in the following section.

Multiprocessing

Using Ruby, you can access UNIX multiprocessing facilities such as `fork`, `exec`, and `wait` as long as the underlying operating system has the necessary facilities to support them. When you call `fork`, the current process splits into two pieces: a `parent` and a `child`. In the `parent`, `fork` returns

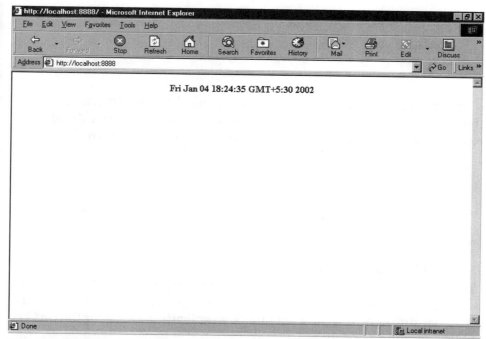

Figure 8.3 Browser output on the client machine.

the process ID of the `child`; in the `child`, it returns `nil`. This is how you can tell which is which. After a `fork`, the two processes can continue to run parts of the same program, as in the following example:

```
if (child = fork)
puts "I'm the parent; the child is #{child}"
else
puts "I'm the child"
end
```

Figure 8.4 shows the output of this code.

```
I am in the child
I am in the parent; the child is 438647
```

Figure 8.4 Code output.

```
I am in the parent the child has process ID 24874
[root@server1 Ruby]# I am the child now executing
exec.rb  wait.rb
```

Figure 8.5   Code output.

Often the reason you wish to `fork` is to run a different program. You can achieve this using `exec`. What this does is replace the currently running program with a different one that you specify. Here is an example:

```
if (child = fork)
puts "I'm the parent; the child has process ID #{child}"
else
puts "I'm the child; now executing ls .."
exec("ls")
end
```

Figure 8.5 shows the output of this code.

This program works fine. However, if the program the `child` runs takes a while to do its work, there is a risk that the `parent` will exit before the `child` has finished. You can avoid this by explicitly waiting for the `child`. Here is a modified version:

```
if (child = fork)
# Wait for the "ls" to complete
Process.wait
# This message is guaranteed to be output after
# the output from ls
puts "I'm the parent; the child has finished"
else
puts "I'm the child; now executing ls .."
exec("ls")
end
```

Figure 8.6 shows the output of this code.

```
I am the child
exec.png  exec.rb  wait.rb
I am the parent the child has finished
```

Figure 8.6   Code output.

Summary

In this chapter, you learned that:

- The pieces of the same program, when run in parallel, are termed as *multithreading* and that, using Ruby, you can implement multithreading.

- You can create a thread by using the method new of the class Thread.

- The Ruby library provides a standard class called TCOServer that handles all the complex details of the underlying operating system. The method new of the class TCPServer accepts two parameters. One is the IP address, and the second is the port number where you want to receive the requests from the client.

- The method Thread.join can be used to suspend the main thread from exiting until all its threads finish executing.

- The method synchronize of the class Mutex can be used by threads to exclusively lock one of the resources.

- You can set a thread to be in a critical state by setting Thread.critical=True.

- You can even set priority to threads by using the priority variable.

- A thread can suspend its own execution by calling the method stop of the class Thread.

- A thread can give control back to the scheduler by calling the method pass of the class Thread.

- A thread can make another thread run by calling the method run of the class Thread.

- You can implement multiprocessing in Ruby by calling the UNIX utilities fork, exec, and wait.

CHAPTER 9

CGI Programming

Getting Started

Web programming is one of the most important application areas of Ruby. Ruby is now fast gaining popularity as an Internet programming language. In the previous chapters you have executed Ruby programs from the command prompt. In this chapter you will learn to execute Ruby programs from a Web browser.

Before beginning, let us check what resources you will need to execute Ruby code from the browser. First of all, you need a computer with Web server software installed. Ruby works well with an Apache Web server. You also need to install Ruby on the Apache Web server. Second, you need a computer that has Web browser software application installed. This computer becomes the client. You will use this client browser to run the Ruby code stored on the Web server. This chapter mainly covers how to write Web-based programs using Ruby. You also will learn about the common gateway interface (CGI). Before you start writing CGI scripts, let us discuss the basics of CGI.

CGI

The Common Gateway Interface (CGI) is a standard for interfacing external applications with information servers, such as Hypertext Transfer Protocol (HTTP) or Web servers. Before the advent of CGI, there were only static Web pages. These Web pages could only provide static information, and no user interaction was possible. Therefore, there arose a need for a specification that would make Web pages interactive. This is precisely where CGI comes into the picture. Consider an example: A database of books exists, and users want to browse through the catalog of books. The browser will send the request to a Web server. The Web server now needs to access the information from the database and send it to the browser. However, the Web server is not familiar with the internals of the database. How will the Web server access the database? Here is where the CGI program provides the connect. The Web server, in turn, executes the CGI script, which is responsible for handling database transactions. The CGI script then passes the database transaction output to the Web server, which in turn passes the output to the client browser. You need to remember that the client browser has no knowledge of the CGI script executed on the Web server.

In Ruby, you write CGI scripts by using the class CGI. The class CGI is a in-built class provided by Ruby. Learning to write CGI scripts requires the knowledge of Hypertext Markup Language (HTML). Therefore, let's revisit some of the concepts related to HTML.

HTML is a language derived from Standard Generalized Markup Language (SGML). HTML has been the principal language for building Web pages for quite some time now. HTML basically consists of tags and elements. In addition, HTML divides a Web page into two parts, the head and the body. The *head* consists of the title of the Web page. The head also contains information regarding communication between the server and the browser. The *body* contains the various elements of the page, such as text, graphics, and animation. Let us see how to represent a simple Web page as a set of HTML tags:

```
<HTML>
<Head>
<Title>Customer information form</Title>
</Head>
<Body bgcolor=#ccffff><pre>
<H1><u> Please enter your details in this form </u></H1>
<Hr>
<Form name=frm1>
First name    <Input type=text name=T1 size=20><br>
Last name     <Input type=text name=T2 size =20><br>
Sex           Male<Input type=Radio name=R1>        Female<Input
type=Radio name=R1>
Home Address          <Input type=text name=T3 size =20><br>
Street                <Input type=text name=T4 size =20><br>
City          <Input type=text name=T5 size =20><br>
State                 <Input type=text name=T6 size =20><br>
Phone                 <Input type=text name=T7 size =20><br>
              <Input type = Submit value="Submit Form">    <Input
type=Reset value="Reset">
</Form></pre>
</Body>
</HTML>
```

The output of this code is an online customer information form with the head (or the title) Customer information form and a body containing the form elements, such as the text box for accepting customer name (Figure 9.1).

Commonly used HTML elements are:

HTML.   The HTML element consists of an opening tag and a closing tag, which are represented as <HTML> and </HTML>, respectively. All the elements of a Web page are enclosed within these two tags. The opening tag indicates the beginning of the Web page, and the closing tag indicates the end of the Web page.

Head.   The Head element represents the title area of the Web page. You represent the Head element between the two tags <Head> and </Head>. The Head element consists of the Title element, which has the title of the Web page. You represent the Title element between the tags <Title> and </Title>.

Body.   The Body element represents the actual contents of the Web page. You represent the Body element between the two tags <Body> and </Body>. All the elements of the Web page are between these two tags.

H1.   The H1 element makes the text appear in the heading 1 font on the Web page. You represent this element between the tags <H1> and </H1>.

hr.   The hr element draws a horizontal line on the Web page. You represent the hr element by using the <hr> tag. No closing tag is required for this element.

Pre.   The Pre element gives the output as specified on the Web page. It can be represented between the tags <Pre> and </Pre>.

Form.   The Form element represents a form on the Web page. You use a form on a Web page to accept data from a user. HTML allows you to enter data in a form with the help of text fields, checkboxes, radio buttons, and list boxes. You represent a form element on a Web page between the tags <Form> and </Form>.

Text field.   The text field allows you to type data in a form. You can use a text field to accept values such as the first name, the last name, the address, the phone number, and the email address. You represent a text field on a Web page with the help of an input tag. The statement <Input type=text name=T1 size =20> represents a text field having the capacity to hold 20 characters and having the name T1. The input tag is part of the form element.

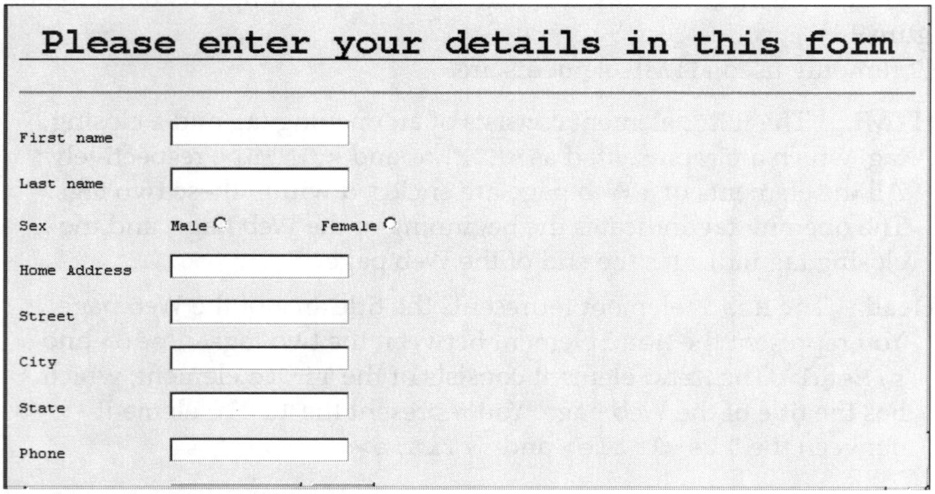

Figure 9.1   Browser output of a Web page.

Radio button. The radio button is used when you want to specify a group of options from which a user should select one. You use radio buttons when you want a user to select an option from a given set of options. The statement `<Input type=radio name=R1>` specifies a radio button named `R1`. All the radio buttons that belong to the same group should have the same name.

Submit button. The submit button submits the data of a form to the Web server. You create a Submit button with the statement `<Input type=submit Value="Submit Form">`. The value `Submit Form` appears on the submit button.

Reset button. The reset button clears the data on a form. You create a reset button with the statement `<Input type=Reset Value="Reset">`. The value `Reset` appears on the reset button.

NOTE The HTML tags are not case-sensitive.

Suppose that you want to display the output `Hello, Welcome to the World of Ruby!!` in a large font. Let us see how to write it first in HTML and then in Ruby:

```
<HTML>
<Head>
<Title> My First page </Title>
</Head>
<Body>
<h1> Hello, Welcome to the World of Ruby!! </h1>
</Body>
</HTML>
```

Now let's see how to write the same code in Ruby:

```
#! /ruby/bin/ruby
print "Content-type:text/html \n\n"
print "<HTML><Head><Title>My First Page</Title></Head>"
print "<Body><h1>Hello, Welcome to the World of
Ruby!!</h1></Body></HTML>"
```

The first line is an important line. The first line of code instructs the Web server about the interpreter to be used to execute the code. Here, `/ruby/bin/ruby` means that the `ruby.exe` file is found in the `bin` directory, which is in the Ruby directory. The Ruby directory, in turn, is in the root directory. The next line, `print "Content-type:text/html \n\n"`, informs the Web server that the following lines of code are either in text or HTML format. The difference between writing HTML code and Ruby code is that HTML code is not executed at the server level. It is executed by the browser, and the output is shown in the browser. However, Ruby code is executed on the Web server, and the output is passed on to the browser and displayed in the browser. Therefore:

```
print "<HTML><Head><Title>My First Page</Title></Head>"
print "<Body><h1>Hello, Welcome to the World of
Ruby!!</h1></Body></HTML>"
```

Here, both the `print` statements are executed on the Web server, and the output of the `print` statements, which is:

```
<HTML><Head><Title>My First Page</Title></Head>
<Body><h1>Hello, Welcome to the World of Ruby!!</h1></Body></HTML>
```

is sent to the browser. The browser then interprets these HTML tags and shows the output.

The question that arises next is how to execute a file on a Web server. Let us discuss the Apache Web server. To execute a file on the Apache Web server, first copy the file in the `cgi-bin` directory, which is in the Apache directory. The Apache directory is placed in the Apache Group directory, which is on the server side. On the client side, you open the browser. On the address bar, you type:

```
http://name/cgi-bin/test.rb
```

where `name` is the name of the Web server, `cgi-bin` is the directory in which you have stored the file, and `test.rb` is the name of the file. The Apache Web server runs the `test.rb` file by using the Ruby interpreter and passes on the output to the browser.

Now let us examine how to write the preceding code using the class `CGI`:

```
#!/ruby/bin/ruby
require 'cgi'
cgi=CGI.new("html3")
cgi.out{
    cgi.html{
            cgi.head{cgi.title{"My First Page"}}
            cgi.body{cgi.h1{"Hello, Welcome to the World of Ruby"}}
            }
    }
```

The first line of the code remains the same as in the preceding code. The next line, `require 'cgi'`, adds the file `cgi.rb` to the code. The code will now be able to access all the classes and methods of the file `cgi.rb`. The next line, `cgi=CGI.new("html3")`, creates a new object of the class CGI. The class CGI has a method for most of the tags. Therefore, `cgi.head`, `cgi.title`, `cgi.body`, and `cgi.h1` will generate the head, title, body, and H1 tags, respectively. The preceding CGI script will generate the HTML tag output shown below and pass the output to the browser.

```
<HTML><Head><Title>My First Page</Title></Head>
<Body><h1>Hello, Welcome to the World of Ruby</h1></Body></HTML>
```

You should notice that the output generated by the Ruby script and the CGI script are the same. These HTML tags are then interpreted by the browser, and the output is as shown in the Figure 9.2.

Capturing HTML Parameters

You must have visited Web sites that ask you for a login name and a password. After you log in, the Web site displays a welcome message and your login name. How is this possible? The only way this can be achieved is that the login page passes on the login name value to the page that displays the welcome message. Therefore, you have the login page, which passes on a parameter, and the welcome page, which traps this parameter value. Passing a parameter can be done easily using HTML forms. Let's learn to trap parameter values using CGI scripts. Consider the following code:

```
#!/ruby/bin/ruby
require 'cgi'
print "Content-type: text/html \n\n"
cgi = CGI.new
print "Name = "
print cgi['Name']
print"<br>"
print"<br>"
print "Type = "
print cgi['Type']
```

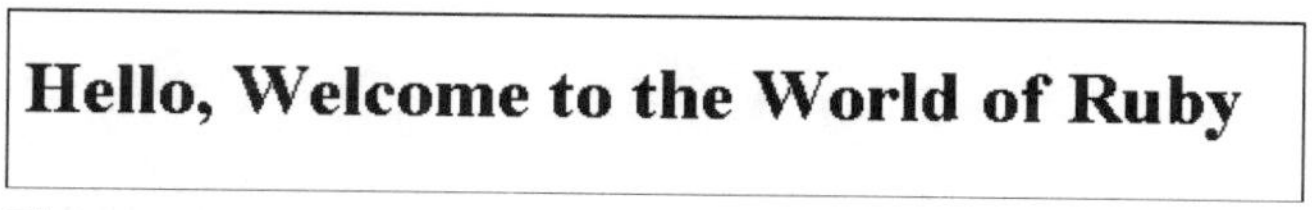

Hello, Welcome to the World of Ruby

Figure 9.2 Browser output.

```
Name = Ruby

Type = Scripting
```

Figure 9.3 Browser output of the CGI code.

This CGI script consists of two parameters, Name and Type. This CGI script expects two values to be passed to it at the time of execution. Let's name this script **cgi.rb**. If you call this script without parameters, you just write http://Apache/cgi-bin/cgi.rb on the address bar of the Web browser, where Apache is the name of the Web server. If you call this script with parameter values, you will need to write http://Apache/cgi-bin/cgi.rb?Name=Ruby&Type=Scripting, where Ruby is the value passed to the Name parameter and Scripting is the value passed to the Type parameter. Therefore, while passing parameters at the time of execution, you need to separate the path of the script from the parameters by using a question mark (?). Then you write:

```
parameter name = parameter value
```

Next, you separate each parameter from the other by using the ampersand operator (&). Figure 9.3 shows the output of the preceding CGI code.

We have discussed how to accept information from a user. The information accepted in a form is mostly stored on the server. However, sometimes storing information on the client computer also helps. Now we will discuss how we can store information on a client computer by using cookies.

Cookies

Cookies are bits of information stored on the client computer by a Web server. When a user requests the same Web page again, the browser passes these bits of information to the Web server along with the request. Using this information, the Web server accordingly responds to the request. These bits of information could be the login name and password of the user, the Internet Protocol (IP) address of the computer, or the time of login. These cookies are stored on the client computer for a certain period of time, after which they are deleted. You will learn how to create these cookies in Ruby. Let's examine the code to create a cookie:

```
#!/ruby/bin/ruby
require 'cgi'
cgi = CGI.new("html3")
```

```ruby
cookieKey = "Knowledge-Inc"
currentCookie = cgi.cookies[cookieKey]
$custID = ""
$visits = 0
if currentCookie.length == 0
     $custID = (999 * rand()).to_i + 1
     $visits = 1
else
     currentCookie.value.each do |item|
             words = item.split("=")
             case words[0]
             when "CustID"
             $custID = words[1]
             when "Visits"
             $visits = words[1].to_i
             end
     end
$visits += 1
end
newCookie = CGI::Cookie.new(cookieKey, "CustID=#{$custID}",
                       "Visits=#{$visits}");
cgi.out( "cookie" => [newCookie]) do
cgi.html do
"\n" +
     cgi.title() do
         "Cookie Test"
     end +
     cgi.center() do
         cgi.h1() do
             "Cookie Test"
         end +
         begin
             if $visits == 1
                 "<b>" +
                 "I see this is your first visit.  Welcome!" +
                 "<p>" +
                 "You have been assigned customer ID #{$custID}." +
                 "</b>"
             else
                 "<b>" +
                 "Welcome back!  This is visit number #{$visits}." +
                 "<p>" +
                 "Your customer ID is #{$custID}." +
                 "</b>"
             end
         end
     end
    end
end
```

This code is a type of cookie test. It checks whether a customer has visited a site before. If a customer is visiting a site for the first time, the code generates a random customer ID for the customer and displays the text `I see this is your first visit. Welcome!`. The code also displays the customer ID. If the customer has visited the site before, the code will display the current number of the visit to the site along with the customer ID.

In the preceding code, notice that you create a cookie by using the following lines:

```
newCookie = CGI::Cookie.new(cookieKey, "CustID=#{$custID}",
                            "Visits=#{$visits}");
```

These lines of code will create a cookie object, `newcookie`. This cookie will be an array that will have values such as `CustID=123 Visits=5`. This means that the customer with customer ID 123 has visited the site five times before and that this is his or her sixth visit. Note that `Cookie` is a class in the CGI module. Figure 9.4 shows the output when a user visits the Web page for the first time, and Figure 9.5 shows the output for a customer who has visited the site before.

Now that you understand the use of cookies, we will discuss how you can use sessions to ensure the security of a Web page.

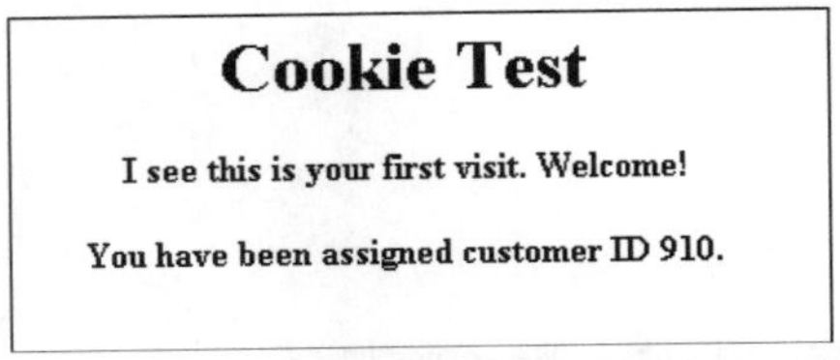

Cookie Test

I see this is your first visit. Welcome!

You have been assigned customer ID 910.

Figure 9.4 Browser output for a new customer.

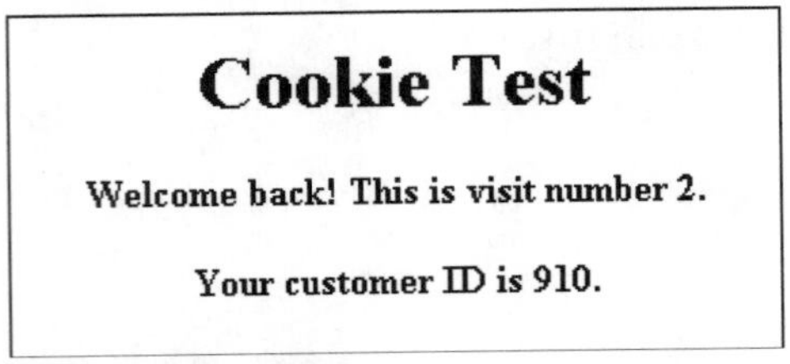

Cookie Test

Welcome back! This is visit number 2.

Your customer ID is 910.

Figure 9.5 Browser output for a customer who has visited the site before.

Sessions

Consider that you are checking your email messages in your company from one of the popular mail Web sites. You log in using your login name and password. You check your email messages and then log off from the Web site. Then you leave your computer unattended. Just imagine that one of your colleagues comes to your computer and clicks the Back button of the browser. The Back button of the browser takes you to the page that was visited last on the browser. This means that the browser will display the page that displayed your email messages. However, this never happens. And this is due to the concept of *sessions*. What happens is that the moment you log into your account, a session is created. This session lasts only until you log out. Therefore, even if somebody tries to access the page by using the Back button, the Web site either displays a page indicating that the session has expired or takes the user back to the login page. Therefore, sessions help you maintain the security of your Web page. You can implement sessions on your Web site using Ruby. Let's see how:

```ruby
#! /ruby/bin/ruby
require 'cgi'
require 'cgi/session'
cgi = CGI.new("html3")
sessionKey = "Knowledge-Inc-Session"
sessionPrefix = "session."
session = CGI::Session.new(cgi, "session_key" => sessionKey,
                           "prefix"        => sessionPrefix)
$lastAccess = session["lastAccess"]
$visits     = session["visits"]
if $visits == nil
    $visits = 1
else
    $visits = $visits.to_i + 1
end
session["visits"] = $visits
session["lastAccess"] = "#{Time.now}"
cgi.out() do
cgi.html do
"\n" +
cgi.title() do
"Session Test"
end +
cgi.center() do
cgi.h1() do
"Session Test"
end +
begin
if $visits == 1
```

```
"<b>" +
"This is your first visit in this session.  Welcome!" +
"</b>"
else
"<b>" +
"This is visit number #{$visits} this session." +
"<p>" +
"Your last access was at #{$lastAccess}<p>" +
"The current time is #{Time.now}" +
"</b>"
end
end
end
end
end
```

The session code is similar to the cookie code. This code also checks whether a customer has visited the site before. However, no customer ID is generated for a new customer. The code displays This is your first visit in this session. Welcome! for a customer visiting the site for the first time. A customer who has visited the site once can see the current number of the visit when he or she visits again. The date and time when the site was last visited and the current date and time also are displayed.

In the preceding code, require 'cgi/session' adds the Session class of the CGI module to the code. This line of code is very important because you will use the method initialize of the class Session to create a session. You create a session by using the following lines:

```
session = CGI::Session.new(cgi, "session_key" => sessionKey,
                       "prefix"      => sessionPrefix)
```

These lines will create a session object called session. Then you create session variables, such as visits and lastAccess, by using session["visits"] and session["lastAccess"].

Until now you have seen how to execute Ruby code from a Web browser. In the preceding examples you created separate files for HTML and Ruby. What if you need to embed Ruby with HTML? To do this, you need to use eRuby as the interpreter. eRuby is discussed in the next section.

eRuby

eRuby is an interpreter for running Ruby code embedded in HTML. Embedded Ruby code in HTML can be compared with Active Server Pages or Java Server Pages. Let's discuss the following code to understand this:

```
#!/ruby/bin/eruby
<html><head><title>eRuby Example</title>
<center><h1>eRuby Example</h1><b>
<% puts "The current time is #{Time.now}" %></b></center>
</head></html>
```

This code consists of HTML tags. You embed the Ruby code in between the HTML tags by using the percent symbol (%). Here you use eRuby as the interpreter. Therefore, you need to provide the proper path for the eruby.exe file:

```
#! /ruby/bin/eruby
```

This code means that the eruby.exe file is in the bin directory, which is in the Ruby directory. The Ruby directory is placed in the root folder. One more important thing you need to remember is to save the file with the .rhtml extension in the cgi-bin directory of the Apache Web server. The expression Time.now displays the current date and time. Even with all this care, you might still come across the terrible screen of Internal Server Error. Then you need to check the httpd.conf file of the Apache Web server. The following two lines need to be present in the httpd.conf file for the eRuby codes to execute:

```
AddType application/x-httpd-eruby .rhtml
Action application/x-httpd-eruby /cgi-bin/eruby
```

Thus, add these two lines in the httpd.conf file and get going. Figure 9.6 shows a simple eRuby program.

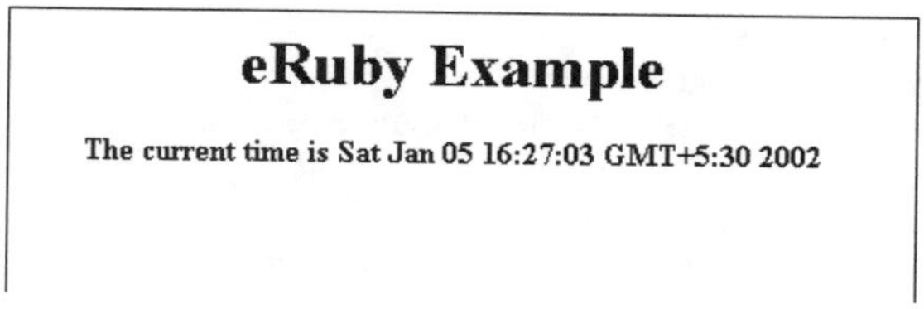

eRuby Example

The current time is Sat Jan 05 16:27:03 GMT+5:30 2002

Figure 9.6 A simple eRuby program.

Creating and Submitting a Form

Problem Statement

The development team of Knowledge, Inc., has been entrusted with the job of creating a page for accepting customer information. This page should accept details such as customer name, age, address, sex, and email address. Once the user clicks on the Submit button, a page should be displayed with all the values entered by the user.

Task List

The tasks that we need to perform for solving this problem are

- ✔ **Create a page in HTML for accepting the customer information.**
- ✔ **Create a CGI script that will display the form values.**
- ✔ **Verify the code.**

Create a Page in HTML for Accepting the Customer Information

Let's examine the HTML code to create a Web page that accepts customer information such as name, age, sex, address, and email address:

```
<HTML>
<Head>
<Title>Form Data</Title>
</Head>
<Body bgcolor=yellow>
<Pre>
<Center><H1><u>Form Data </u></H1></Center>
<b><Form name="frm1" action="cgi_action.rb">
Name          <input type=text name="Name">
Age           <input type=text name="Age">
Address       <input type=textarea name="Address">
Sex           M <Input type=radio name="Sex">     F <Input type=radio
name="Sex">
E-mail address       <input type=text name="E-mail">
              <Input type="submit" Name="Submit" value="SUBMIT">
```

```
</b></Form></Pre>
</Body>
</HTML>
```

Create a CGI Script that Will Display the Form Values

In the form, you have a Submit button to submit the values of the form to the Web server. Here is where the CGI script comes into picture. The CGI script always resides on the server. Clicking the Submit button invokes the specified CGI script on the server. In this example, the CGI script `cgi_action.rb` is invoked. This CGI script then handles the form data. Mostly, CGI script takes care of storing the form data in the database. Here the CGI script will dynamically create an HTML page displaying the customer details:

```ruby
#! /ruby/bin/ruby
require 'cgi'
print "Content-type: text/html\r\n\r\n"
cgi=CGI.new
print "Name = "
print cgi['Name']
print "<br>"
print "<br>"
print "Age = "
print cgi['Age']
print "<br>"
print "<br>"
print "Address = "
print cgi['Address']
print "<br>"
print "<br>"
print "Sex = "
print cgi['Sex']
print "<br>"
print "<br>"
print "E-mail Address = "
print cgi['E-mail']
```

Verify the Code

Enter the values in the HTML page, and click the Submit button. Check whether an HTML page is generated and also check whether the values displayed are the same as entered in the form (Figure 9.7).

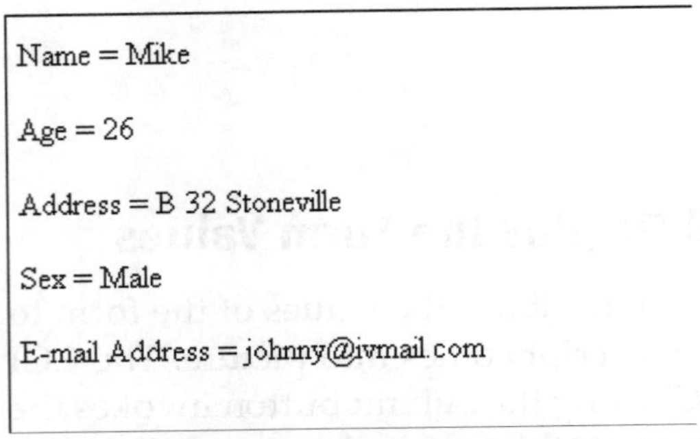

Name = Mike

Age = 26

Address = B 32 Stoneville

Sex = Male

E-mail Address = johnny@ivmail.com

Figure 9.7   The HTML page generated by the CGI script.

Summary

In this chapter you learned:

- The basics of HTML by creating a simple HTML page for accepting values from a user.
- How to create CGI scripts using the class CGI.
- How to execute Ruby codes on a Web server using a client machine browser.
- How to pass parameters at the time of execution of the CGI script.
- That whenever you visit a Web page, the Web site stores some bits of information in your machine. These bits of information are called *cookies*. The Web server uses these cookies the next time you visit the site.
- How to implement sessions using Ruby.
- How to embed Ruby codes in HTML using the % tags. You save the file with a .rhtml extension and execute the file from the Web browser. You need to remember to provide the path of the eruby.exe file in the code.
- How to write CGI scripts that accept values from the form and generates an HTML page that displays the entered values.

GUI Programming with Tk

OBJECTIVES

In this chapter you will learn to:

✔ Identify the significance of the Tk module

✔ Identify the steps to create a GUI application

✔ Identify the widgets provided by the Tk module

✔ Use various widgets in your application

Getting Started

Until now, the chapters in this book have discussed how to create applications that work on the command-line interface. You executed Ruby scripts and viewed their output at the command prompt. If the application required user input, you entered the input at the prompt.

At times, text-based applications can be very monotonous for a user and difficult to work with. This chapter can be helpful for those who want to learn to develop user-friendly graphic interfaces. Imagine how exciting it would be to enable a user to enter the required details in a window with different controls for each detail where the user can activate or choose options simply by pointing and clicking with a mouse instead of asking for details on the Ruby prompt. Such applications that interact with a user by means of an interface represented by using icons, menus, and dialog boxes on the screen are called *graphic user interface* (GUI) applications.

In this chapter you will learn about Tk, the GUI framework for Ruby, and use Tk to create GUI applications. As a part of this, you will learn about various controls that can be included in a GUI. You will further enhance the skills you gain in this chapter by designing a GUI application. Before moving on to the concepts related to Tk, let's take a brief overview of GUI applications.

A GUI application has a user interface. We can compare this with a painting. In the case of a painting, the canvas holds together various components, such as lines, circles, and boxes. Similarly, a GUI application consists of a number of controls, such as text boxes, labels, and buttons, that are contained inside a window. You no doubt have come across a number of GUI applications in day-to-day life. These applications can range from an online registration form on a Web site to a calculator used in a home personal computer (PC).

Ruby enables you to create visually appealing GUI applications using Tk. The next section discusses Tk.

Introduction to Tk

Tk is the standard GUI library for Ruby. When combined with Tk, Ruby provides a fast and easy way to create GUI applications. Tk provides a powerful object-oriented interface to the Tk GUI toolkit. Tk provides various controls, such as buttons, labels, and text boxes, in a GUI application. These controls are commonly called *widgets*.

As mentioned earlier, creating a GUI application using Tk is an easy task. All you need to do is perform the following steps:

1. Load the Tk module.
2. Create the GUI application window.

3. Add widgets to the GUI application.

4. Enter the main event loop.

Let's now elaborate on how to perform these steps.

Loading the Tk Module

The Tk module contains all the classes and widgets required to create a GUI application. To use this module in your application, you need to add it to the application. The following code statement will help you load the Tk module:

```
require Tk
```

Creating the GUI Application Window

Any GUI application should first contain a top-level window, or a *root window,* that can further contain the various objects required in the application. The objects contained in the root window could be widgets, such as buttons and labels, or other windows. To create a root window for your application, use the following statement:

```
top = Tkroot.new
```

The method new of the class Tkroot creates a root window for the application and returns the reference of the window, which in this case is assigned to the variable top.

Adding Widgets to the Application

Using Tk, you can add a number of widgets to your Ruby application. These widgets can be stand-alone widgets or containers. *Stand-alone widgets* are the ones that do not contain any other widgets, such as buttons, checkboxes, and labels. *Container widgets* are the ones that contain other widgets, such as frames and windows. A container widget is also called a *parent widget*, and a contained widget is called a *child widget*. Various widgets provided by Tk are listed in Table 10.1. You will learn to add widgets to your application later in this chapter.

Table 10.1 Widgets Provided by Tk

WIDGETS	DESCRIPTION
Button	The Button widget is used to display buttons in an application.
Canvas	The Canvas widget is used to draw shapes, such as lines, ovals, polygons, and rectangles, in an application.
Checkbutton	The Checkbutton widget is used to display a number of options as checkboxes. The user can select multiple options at a time.
Entry	The Entry widget is used to display a single-line text field for accepting values from a user.
Frame	The Frame widget is used as a container widget to organize other widgets.
Label	The Label widget is used to provide a single-line caption for other widgets. It also can contain images.
Listbox	The Listbox widget is used to provide a list of options to a user.
Menubutton	The Menubutton widget is used to display menus in an application.
Menu	The Menu widget is used to provide various commands in a menu.
Message	The Message widget is used to display a multiline text field for accepting values from a user.
Radiobutton	The Radiobutton widget is used to display a number of options as radio buttons. The user can select only one option at a time.
Scale	The Scale widget is used to provide a slider widget.
Scrollbar	The Scrollbar widget is used to add scrolling capability to various widgets, such as list boxes.
Text	The Text widget is used to display text in multiple lines.
Toplevel	The Toplevel widget is used to provide a separate window container.

Entering the Main Event Loop

After you design an application by adding appropriate widgets, you need to execute the application. When an application is executed, it enters an infinite loop. This loop includes waiting for an event, such as a mouse click; processing the event; and then waiting for the next event. The statement that helps your application enter the infinite loop is:

```
Tk.mainloop()
```

Let's put the pieces together and consolidate the code to display a window using the Tk module:

```
require 'Tk'
  #Code to add widgets
Tk.mainloop()
```

The output of this code is shown in Figure 10.1.

Now that you understand the basic steps involved in creating a GUI application using Tk, let's create a GUI application.

Creating a GUI Application

Problem Statement

The management of Knowledge, Inc., wants a form to be designed that will accept customer details and the details of the book to be purchased. Mike, the project leader, knows that Ruby works well with Tk. He wants his team to create a sample form that will accept details such as first name, last name, age, and gender from the customer. The form also should display a list of sample books in a listbox. When the user clicks on a Submit button, a message box should be displayed indicating the chosen option.

Figure 10.1   A sample window.

Task List

Based on the problem statement, the following tasks can be identified:

- ✔ **Identify the components of the user interface of the form.**
- ✔ **Identify the Tk elements to design the user interface.**
- ✔ **Write the code for the user interface.**
- ✔ **Execute the code.**

Identify the Components of the User Interface

The user-interface form should have the following components to gather the required information from customers:

- Two text boxes to accept the customer name. The first text box will accept the first name, and the second text box will accept the last name.
- A text box to accept the age of the customer.
- Radio buttons to accept the gender of the customer.
- A list of sample books.
- A Submit button.

Identify the Tk Widgets to Design the User Interface

Table 10.2 describes the Tk widgets to be used for design of the form. Let's now look at the details of these components.

Table 10.2 Widgets to Be Used in the Window

WIDGET	PURPOSE
Label	To provide captions for various widgets
Entry	To display a single-line entry field for accepting values, such as the first name and the last name
Listbox	To display the list of sample books
Radiobutton	To accept the gender of a customer
Button	To display a message box

The Label Widget

The Label widget is used to display text or provide captions for other widgets. For example, you can use a label to provide captions for various other widgets present in a window. In addition, you can display bitmaps and images in a label. Use the following syntax to display a text label in a window:

```
lb1=TkLabel.new(top){
text 'Hello World'
pack()
}
```

This code creates a label with the text Hello World (Figure 10.2). In the preceding code:

- A label is created by using the method new of the class TkLabel. Here, top refers to the window on which the label is to be displayed.

- The text option is used to specify the text to be displayed in the label.

- The method pack is used to display the position of the label in the window. You will learn more about the method pack later in this chapter.

Table 10.3 lists some other options that you can use with a Label widget. The following code statement implements some of these options of the Label widget:

```
lb1=TkLabel.new(top){
text 'Hello World'
background "yellow"
foreground "blue"
pack()
}
```

Figure 10.2 A sample window displaying a label.

Table 10.3 Various Options of the **Label** Widget

OPTION	DESCRIPTION
bitmap	Specifies the bitmap to be displayed
borderwidth	Specifies the width of the label border
background	Specifies the background color of the label
foreground	Specifies the color of the text present in the label
font	Specifies the font of the text to be displayed
justify	Specifies the alignment of multiple lines of text, with values such as left, right, or center

The Entry Widget

The Entry widget is used to accept single-line text strings from a user. Let's now look at the syntax to display an Entry widget in an application:

```
e1 = TkEntry.new(top)
e1.pack()
```

Like the Label widget, you can use various options with the Entry widget. Some of these options are listed in Table 10.4. The following code statement implements some of these options of the Entry widget, and Figure 10.3 shows a sample window displaying an Entry widget.

```
e1 = TkEntry.new(top){
background "red"
foreground "blue"
pack()
}
```

Table 10.4 Various Options of the **Entry** Widget

OPTION	DESCRIPTION
borderwidth	Specifies the width of the Entry widget border
background	Specifies the background color of the Entry widget
foreground	Specifies the color of the text in the Entry widget
font	Specifies the font of the text in the text field
relief	Specifies the type of the border, with such values as flat, groove, raised, ridge, or sunken

Figure 10.3 A sample window displaying an `Entry` widget.

Following is the complete code to display a `label` and an `Entry` widget:

```
require 'tk'
top = TkRoot.new {title "Label and Entry Widget"}
#code to add a label widget
lb1 = TkLabel.new(top){
text 'Hello World'
background "yellow"
foreground "blue"
pack()
}
#code to add a entry widget
e1 = TkEntry.new(top){
background "red"
foreground "blue"
pack()
}
Tk.mainloop
```

Figure 10.4 shows the output of this code.

In addition to these options, an Entry widget also provides a number of methods. Table 10.5 lists some of these methods.

Figure 10.4 A sample window displaying a `label` and an `Entry` widget.

Table 10.5   Various Methods to Manipulate the `Entry` Widget

METHOD	FUNCTION	EXAMPLE
`insert(index, text)`	This method inserts text at the given index. Some of the values used to specify index are `insert` and `end`.	`E1.insert( 'insert', "Hello")` This statement inserts `Hello` at the current cursor position.
`delete(index)`	This method deletes the character at the specified index.	`E1.delete(1)` This statement deletes the character at the index position `1`.
`delete(from, to)`	This method deletes the characters within the specified range.	`E1.delete(0, END)` This statement deletes all the characters present in a string.
`get()`	This method retrieves the contents present in the text field.	`E1.get()` This statement returns the contents of the `E1` widget.

You can see in Figure 10.4 that the widgets are randomly placed in the window. This is so because we did not arrange the widgets in the parent window. Tk provides you with various classes to help you organize the placement of widgets in a window. These classes are also called *geometry managers*.

Geometry Managers

Widgets in a window should be in proper layout so that they do not appear scattered. In Ruby, *geometry management* is the technique used to organize widgets in their container widget. Tk provides a powerful and flexible model to manage the placement of widgets in a container.

To organize various widgets inside a window or another widget, Tk provides three classes or geometry managers: `pack`, `grid`, and `place`. Let's discuss these geometry managers briefly.

- The `pack` geometry manager organizes widgets in rows or columns inside the parent window or the widget. To manage widgets easily, the `pack` geometry manager provides various options, such as `fill`, `expand`, and `side`.

- The `fill` option is used to specify whether a widget should occupy all the space given to it by the parent window or the widget. Some of the possible values that can be used with this option are `none`, `x`, `y`, or `both`. By default, the `fill` option is set to `none`.

- The `expand` option is used to specify whether a widget should expand to fill any extra space available. The default value is `0`, which means that the widget is not expanded. The other value is `1`.

- The `side` option is used to specify the side against which the widget is to be packed. Some of the possible values that can be used with this option are `top`, `left`, `bottom`, or `right`. By default, the widgets are packed against the `top` edge of the parent window.

- Let's now rewrite the code to display the `Label` and an `Entry` widget that we discussed in the preceding section using the `pack` geometry manager:

```
require 'tk'
top = TkRoot.new {title "Label and Entry Widget"}
#code to add a label widget
lb1=TkLabel.new(top){
text 'Hello World'
background "yellow"
foreground "blue"
pack('padx'=>10, 'pady'=>10, 'side'=>'left')
}
#code to add a entry widget
e1 = TkEntry.new(top){
background "red"
foreground "blue"
pack('padx'=>10, 'pady'=>10, 'side'=>'left')
}
Tk.mainloop
```

- When you execute this code, a window containing both the widgets appears, as shown in Figure 10.5.

Figure 10.5 Organizing widgets by using the `pack` geometry manager.

- The `grid` geometry manager is the most flexible and easy-to-use geometry manager. It logically divides the parent window or the widget into rows and columns in a two-dimensional table. You can then place a widget in an appropriate row and column format by using the `row` and `column` options, respectively. To understand the use of `row` and `column` options, consider the following code:

```
require 'tk'
top = TkRoot.new {title "Label and Entry Widget"}
#code to add a label widget
lb1=TkLabel.new(top){
text 'Hello World'
background "yellow"
foreground "blue"
grid('row'=>0, 'column'=>0)
}
#code to add a entry widget
e1 = TkEntry.new(top){
background "red"
foreground "blue"
grid('row'=>0, 'column'=>1)
}
Tk.mainloop
```

When you execute this code, a window containing both the widgets appears, as shown in Figure 10.6.

- The `place` geometry manager allows you to place a widget at the specified position in the window. You can specify the position either in absolute terms or relative to the parent window or the widget. To specify an absolute position, use the `x` and `y` options. To specify a position relative to the parent window or the widget, use the `relx` and `rely` options. In addition, you can specify the relative size of the widget by using the `relwidth` and `relheight` options provided by this geometry manager.

Figure 10.6 Organizing widgets by using the grid geometry manager.

Let's now look at the code to implement the `place` geometry manager:

```
require 'tk'
top = TkRoot.new {title "Label and Entry Widget"}
#code to add a label widget
lb1=TkLabel.new(top){
text 'Hello World'
background "yellow"
foreground "blue"
place('relx'=>0.0,'rely'=>0.0)
}
#code to add a entry widget
e1 = TkEntry.new(top){
background "red"
foreground "blue"
place('relx'=>0.4,'rely'=>0.0)
}
Tk.mainloop
```

When you execute this code, a window containing both the widgets appears, as shown in Figure 10.7.

Figure 10.7   Organizing widgets by using the `place` geometry manager.

The Button Widget

The Button widget is used to add buttons in a Ruby application. These buttons can display either text or images that convey the purpose of the buttons. You can attach a function or a method to a button, which is called automatically when you click the button. Consider the following statement that is used to display a button:

```
b1=TkButton.new(top){
text "submit"
command proc{lb1.configure('background'=>'red')}
pack()
}
```

In this code:

- top represents the parent window.
- The text option is used to specify the text to be displayed on the button.
- The command option is used to specify the function or procedure that is called when a user clicks the button. In this case, the method configure of the Label widget is called. You can set the options of a widget by using the method configure.

Table 10.6 lists some of the options that can be used with the Button widget, and Figure 10.8 shows a sample window.

Table 10.6 Various Options of the Button Widget

OPTION	DESCRIPTION
background	Specifies the background color of the button
foreground	Specifies the color of the text in the button
font	Specifies the font of the text.
relief	Specifies the type of the border, such as flat, groove, raised, ridge, and sunken
image	Specifies the image to be displayed in the button
width, height	Specify the size of the button

Figure 10.8 A sample window containing a button.

The Listbox Widget

The Listbox widget is used to display a list of items from which a user can select a number of items. To create a list box in your application, use the following syntax:

```
list1 = TkListbox.new(top){
pack()
}
```

This code creates a blank list box, as shown in Figure 10.9. Therefore, you need to add items to it. To do so, you use the method insert. The syntax of this method is:

```
list1.insert(index, item)
```

In this syntax:

- index refers to the index position at which an item is to be inserted. Some of the possible values of an index are insert and end. The insert value places the item at the current cursor position, and the end value places the item at the end.

- item refers to the value to be inserted and can be of the text type only.

For example:

```
list1.insert('end', "Rose")
```

inserts the item Rose at the end of the List1 list box.
Let's now write a complete code to insert a list box in a window:

```
require 'tk'
list1 = TkListbox.new(top)
list1.insert(1,"Python")
list1.insert(2,"Perl")
list1.insert(3,"C")
list1.insert(4,"PHP")
list1.insert(5,"JSP")
list1.insert(6,"Ruby")
list1.pack()
Tk.mainloop
```

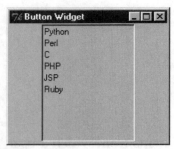

Figure 10.9 A window containing the Listbox widget.

This code creates a Listbox widget containing the names of different languages at the specified indices, as shown in Figure 10.9.

The Listbox widget provides a number of other methods that make it easy to work with this widget. Some of these methods are listed in Table 10.7.

Table 10.7 Methods Provided by the Listbox Widget

METHOD	FUNCTION	EXAMPLE
curselection()	This method retrieves the index position of the selected index.	Lb1.curselection() This statement returns the index position of the currently selected item.
delete(index)	This method deletes the item at the specified index.	Lb1.delete(1) This statement deletes the item at index position 1.
delete(first, last)	This method deletes the items within the specified range. For example, you can use 0, 'end' to delete all the items in the list.	Lb1.delete(0, 'end') This statement deletes all the items present in the list box.
get(index)	This method retrieves the item present at the specified index.	E1.get(1) This statement returns the item present at index position 1 of the list box.

The CheckButton Widget

The CheckButton widget is used to display a number of options to a user as toggle buttons. The user can then select one or more options by clicking the button corresponding to each option. You also can display images in the place of text. The syntax to display a checkbutton in an application is as follows:

```
checkVar=TkVariable.new
c1 = TkCheckButton.new(top){
text "Music"
variable checkVar
pack()
}
```

In this syntax:

- ■ top refers to the parent window.
- ■ The text option specifies the text to be displayed.
- ■ The variable option attaches a Tk variable (checkVar) to the checkbutton. You create a Tk variable by using the method new of class TkVariable. When you click the button, the value contained in the variable is toggled between the on value and the off value, which specifies whether the button is checked or unchecked. You can set these values by using the onvalue and offvalue options.

The preceding code creates a checkbutton Music, as shown in Figure 10.10. Table 10.8 lists some of the methods that you can use with a checkbutton.

Figure 10.10   A window containing a Checkbutton widget.

Table 10.8 Methods Provided by the `Checkbutton` Widget

METHOD	FUNCTION	EXAMPLE
deselect()	To deselect the button	C1.deselect()
select()	To select the button	C1.deselect()
toggle()	To reverse the toggle state of the button	C1.toggle()

The RadioButton Widget

Like the CheckButton widget, the RadioButton widget is also used to display a number of options to a user as toggle buttons. However, a user can select only one option at a time. The syntax to display a radio button is:

```
require 'Tk'
top = TkRoot.new{title "Radio Button"}
radioVar=TkVariable.new
r1 = TkRadioButton.new(top){
text "Male"
variable radioVar
value 1
}
r1.pack()
r2 = TkRadioButton.new(top){
text "Female"
variable radioVar
value 2
}
r2.pack()
Tk.mainloop
```

This code creates two radio buttons, Male and Female, as shown in Figure 10.11. You need to add these buttons to one group so that a user can select only one of them at a time. To do so, ensure that the variable option points to the same variable name (radioVar).

Like the CheckButton widget, a RadioButton widget also supports the methods select() and deselect(). These methods are used to select and deselect the button, respectively.

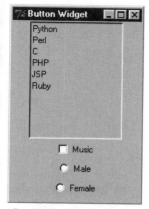

Figure 10.11   A window containing a `RadioButton` widget.

The Frame Widget

The `Frame` widget is a container widget that is used to organize other widgets. *Frame* refers to a rectangular area on a parent window. To understand the use of the `Frame` widget, consider a situation where you need to add a number of radio buttons to your application. Organizing a large number of radio buttons in the parent window is a tedious task. Therefore, to simplify this process, you can add all the radio buttons to a frame and then add the frame to the parent window. The syntax to create a frame is:

```
f1 = TkFrame.new(top){
width 100
height 100
}
```

This code creates a frame of the size specified using the `width` and `height` options. This frame is created in the `top` window.

The following code demonstrates the process of adding widgets to a frame:

```
v = TkVariable.new
r1=TkRadioButton.new(f1){
text "Male"
```

```
variable v
value 1
}
r2=TkRadiobutton.new(f1){
text "Female"
variable v
value 2
}
```

Write the Code for the User Interface

After identifying the widgets required to design the user interface, write the code for the user interface. Thus:

```
require 'tk'
top=TkRoot.new{title "Shopping Details"}
fname_label=TkLabel.new(top){
text "First Name"
place('relx'=>0.0,'rely'=>0.1)
}
fname_entry=TkEntry.new(top){
place('relx'=>0.1,'rely'=>0.1)
}
lname_label=TkLabel.new(top){
text "Last Name"
place('relx'=>0.0,'rely'=>0.2)
}
lname_entry=TkEntry.new(top){
place('relx'=>0.1,'rely'=>0.2)
}
age_label=TkLabel.new(top){
text "Age"
place('relx'=>0.0,'rely'=>0.3)
}
age_entry=TkEntry.new(top){
place('relx'=>0.1,'rely'=>0.3)
}
gender_label=TkLabel.new(top){
text "Gender : "
place('relx'=>0.0,'rely'=>0.4)
}
radioVar=TkVariable.new
r1 = TkRadioButton.new(top){
text "Male"
variable radioVar
```

```
value 1
place('relx'=>0.1,'rely'=>0.4)
}
r2 = TkRadioButton.new(top){
text "Female"
variable radioVar
value 2
place('relx'=>0.2,'rely'=>0.4)
}
list = TkListbox.new(top){
place('relx'=>0.8,'rely'=>0.1)
}
list.insert(1,"Python")
list.insert(2,"Perl")
list.insert(3,"C")
list.insert(4,"PHP")
list.insert(5,"JSP")
list.insert(6,"Ruby")
submit=TkButton.new(top){
text "SUBMIT"
command proc {
val=list.curselection()
sel = list.get(val)
Tk.messageBox('message'=>"The book name chosen is #{sel} ")
}
place('relx'=>0.3,'rely'=>0.8)
}
Tk.mainloop
```

To display the message box, you can use the method `Tk.messageBox`. The `message` argument of the method contains the message to be displayed in the message box.

Execute the Code

1. Save the file as `sample.rb`, and execute it at the command prompt. A window appears as shown in Figure 10.12.

2. In the window that appears, enter the following details:

   - First name: John

   - Last name: Smith

   - Age: 21

   - Gender: Male

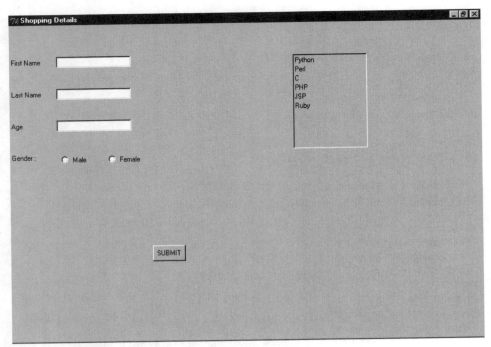

Figure 10.12   Sample form.

3. Select `Perl` from the list of the books, and click the Submit button. A message box appears as shown in Figure 10.13.

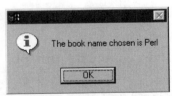

Figure 10.13   Message box displaying the name of the book.

Summary

In this chapter you learned that:

- The `Tk` module is a collection of classes that help you create GUI applications in Ruby.
- The steps involved in creating a GUI application using Tk are as follows:
  - Add the `Tk` module.
  - Create the application window.
  - Add widgets to the application.
  - Enter the main event loop.
- The `Label` widget is used to display text.
- The `Entry` widget is used to accept single-line text strings from a user.
- The `Button` widget is used to display various types of buttons.
- The `Listbox` widget is used to display a list of items from which a user can select one or more items.
- The `CheckButton` widget is used to display a number of options to a user as a toggle buttons. A user can select more than one option by clicking the buttons corresponding to the selected options.
- The `RadioButton` widget is also used to display a number of options to a user as toggle buttons. However, a user can select only one option at a time.
- The `Frame` widget is the container widget that is used to organize other widgets.

CHAPTER

11

Running Ruby on Windows

OBJECTIVES

In this chapter you will learn:

- ✔ **How Ruby runs on Windows**
- ✔ **About the advantage of using the** `rubyw.exe` **file**
- ✔ **About the class** `Win32API`
- ✔ **How to use Windows automation features in Ruby**

Getting Started

This book primarily covers how Ruby behaves in a Windows environment. However, Ruby actually was created for POSIX environments. Therefore, Ruby can easily access the system features in POSIX environments. At this point, you might wonder how Ruby works in Windows because Windows does not provide a POSIX environment. Let's see how this is possible.

Ruby and Windows

When you download and run the one-click setup file for Ruby in Windows, the setup file installs a `Cygwin.DLL` file. This creates a simulation of the POSIX environment in Windows. Using this simulation, Ruby works efficiently in Windows. When you install Ruby, various `.exe` files are copied in the `bin` directory. One of these `.exe` files is `rubywin.exe`. Rubywin, created by Masaki Suketa, provides a complete Integrated Development Environment (IDE) for Ruby on a Windows platform. If you do not have Rubywin, you can download it from the Ruby Application Archive. Rubywin is very simple to use. The other `.exe` files that will be of interest to you are `ruby.exe`, `eruby.exe`, and `rubyw.exe`. The `ruby.exe` file is used to run `.rb` files. The `eruby.exe` file is used to run `.rhtml` files. You have learned about `ruby.exe` and `eruby.exe`. Let us see how to use `rubyw.exe`.

The `rubyw.exe` file is used to execute `.rbw` files. You may want to know what a `.rbw` file is. A `.rbw` file is similar to a `.rb` file. You can save all the `.rb` files with the `.rbw` extension. You might have noticed that when you double-click a `.rb` file, a command window pops up and remains open until the program stops. As soon as the program stops, the command window closes. However, when you run a `.rbw` file, no command window opens, and the program runs in the background. This can be especially useful when you are trying to run a Web server application. Double-click on that file. You will notice that a command window opens. It does not close because the code is still running. If you try to close the window, the Web server stops execution. Now save `Webserver.rb` as `Webserver.rbw` and double-click that file. You will notice that the Web server has started, but no window opens. The Web service is running in the background. This is the advantage of `.rbw` files.

Windows automation is another feature supported by Ruby. To use Windows automation, you require a client and an automation server such as Microsoft Word, Excel, or PowerPoint. You can access the Microsoft office features from the automation client. Ruby can act as an automation client. Let's discuss how to use automation in Ruby by taking the problem statement of Knowledge, Inc.

Using WIN32OLE

Problem Statement

The management of Knowledge Inc. a book publishing company, wants to conduct a study to determine the company's place in the market in relation to its competitors. The competitors are Portland Books, Oceanic Inc., and Learn2grow.com. Management wants to compare the annual revenues and annual profits of Knowledge Inc., against the annual revenues and profits of the competitors depicted in an Excel chart format. The development team is enthusiastic about learning Ruby. Therefore, management wants the team to use automation in Ruby and create these Excel charts from Ruby. Management also wants these data to be stored into a Word document for reference.

Task List

- ✔ **Write the code to create a chart in Excel.**
- ✔ **Write the code to insert data into Word.**
- ✔ **Save and execute the code.**

Write the Code to Create a Chart in Excel

To use the automation features, Ruby provides a class WIN32OLE. To access the automation server features, you need to create an object of the class WIN32OLE. Let's examine the process to do this:

```
excelobj = WIN32OLE.new("excel.application")
```

This would create a WIN32OLE object excelobj for the Microsoft Excel automation server. Similarly, you can create Microsoft Word and PowerPoint objects like this:

```
wordobj = WIN32OLE.new("word.application")
powerobj = WIN32OLE.new("powerpoint.application")
```

To access WIN32OLE methods, you need to first include the class WIN32OLE. You can do this by using the require statement:

```
require 'win32ole'
```

This statement will allow you to access all the methods of the class WIN32OLE.

The class WIN32OLE has such methods as new and invoke. The method new, as we know, is used to create a WIN32OLE object. The method invoke is used to handle all the methods unknown to the class WIN32OLE. For example, consider this statement:

```
excelobj['Visible']=TRUE
```

This statement is very important to start a particular application. However, the class WIN32OLE does not recognize the method Visible. Therefore, the method invoke handles such methods. We know that Microsoft Excel consists of workbooks and worksheets. After you have started the Microsoft Excel application, you need to add a workbook to it. You can do this by typing:

```
excelobj.workbooks.add()
```

This statement adds a workbook to the application. Now you can work with the workbook. In the same way, you need to add documents to the Microsoft Word application:

```
wordobj.documents.add()
```

To add values in the cells in Microsoft Excel, you use the method Range. You can add a value, say, 100, to the cell A6 by using the following statement:

```
excelobj.Range("a6")['Value'] = 100
```

You can use the method select to select a range of cells. Consider a set of the four cells, a1, a2, a3, and a4, with the values 100, 200, 300, and 400, respectively. Let's learn to use the method select:

```
excelobj.Range("a1")['Value'] = 100
excelobj.Range("a2")['Value'] = 200
excelobj.Range("a3")['Value'] = 300
excelobj.Range("a4")['Value'] = 400
excelobj.Range("a1:a4").select()
```

This would select the range of cells from a1 to a4.

Let us implement our learning of automation to create a chart in Excel to address the problem of the Knowledge, Inc., management. Thus:

```
require 'win32ole'
puts "Graphical representation of the annual revenues and profits made
in the year 2001 by Portland books, Oceanic Inc, Learn2Grow.com, and
Knowledge Inc. "
puts "Enter the revenue of Portland books in millions"
portland_revenue=gets
puts "Enter the revenue of Oceanic Inc. in millions"
oceanic_revenue=gets
puts "Enter the revenue of Learn2Grow in millions"
learn_revenue=gets
puts "Enter the revenue of Knowledge Inc. in millions"
knowledge_revenue=gets
puts "enter the profits of the four companies"
puts "Enter the profit for Portland books"
portland_profit=gets
puts "Enter the profit for Oceanic Inc."
oceanic_profit=gets
puts "Enter the profit for Learn2Grow.com"
learn_profit=gets
puts "Enter the profit for Knowledge Inc."
knowledge_profit=gets
excel=WIN32OLE.new("excel.application")
excel['Visible']=TRUE
workbook=excel.workbooks.add()
excel.Range("a1")['Value']=portland_revenue
excel.Range("a2")['Value']=oceanic_revenue
excel.Range("a3")['Value']=learn_revenue
excel.Range("a4")['Value']=knowledge_revenue
excel.Range("a1:a4").select()
excel.Range("b1")['Value']=portland_profit
excel.Range("b2")['Value']=oceanic_profit
excel.Range("b3")['Value']=learn_profit
excel.Range("b4")['Value']=knowledge_profit
excel.Range("b1:b4").select()
excelchart1=workbook.charts.add()
excelchart2=workbook.charts.add()
excelchart1['Type']=-4099
excelchart2['Type']=-4099
workbook.SaveAs "Graph.xls"
excel.Quit
```

In this code we have created two bar graphs. One bar graph is used to compare revenues, and the other bar graph is used to compare profits. The code accepts the values for the revenues and profits from the user and then inserts the values into Microsoft Excel cells. Then the code selects the range of cells based on what you need to create a chart. For example, the cells from a1 to a4 are selected to create a revenue chart, and the cells from b1 to b4 are selected to create a profit chart.

You can create a chart with this code:

```
excelchart1 = workbook.charts.add()
```

This statement would create a chart object excelchart1. You also need to specify the type of chart you require. Each chart in Excel has a constant number assigned to it. For example, an xl3Dbar chart has the constant -4099 assigned to it. You can take a look at the Excel chart constants specified below:

```
xlRadar = -4151
xlXYScatter = -4169
xlCombination = -4111
xl3DArea = -4098
xl3DBar = -4099
xl3DColumn = -4100
xl3DLine = -4101
xl3DPie = -4102
xl3DSurface = -4103
xlDoughnut = -4120
```

You can specify a type for an Excel chart by:

```
excelchart1['Type']=-4099
```

You can use the method SaveAs of the workbook to save the Excel workbook. In the preceding code we have assigned our workbook to the object workbook. Therefore, we can write the following:

```
Workbook.SaveAs "Graph.xls"
```

This workbook would be saved in the default folder mentioned in the Default File Location text box on the General tab of the Options dialog box. You can access the Options dialog box by choosing Options from the Tools menu.

You quit the application by using the Quit statement:

```
excel.Quit
```

Write the Code to Insert Data into Word

```
word=WIN32OLE.new("word.application")
word['Visible']=TRUE
worddoc=word.documents.add()
worddoc.Content.Text="
Portland Books
Revenue:      #{portland_revenue}
Profits:      #{portland_profit}
Oceanic Inc.
Revenue:      #{oceanic_revenue}
profits:      #{oceanic_profit}
Learn2Grow.com
Revenue:      #{learn_revenue}
profits:      #{learn_profit}
Knowledge Inc.
Revenue:      #{knowledge_revenue}
profits:      #{knowledge_profit}
worddoc.SaveAs "Graph.doc"
worddoc.close
```

This code inserts the profits and revenues of all four companies.

If you want the text ABC to be inserted in the Word document, write the following:

```
wordobj = WIN32OLE.new("word.application")
worddoc = wordobj.documents.add()
worddoc.Content.Text="ABC"
```

Save and Execute the Code

Save the code as Graph.rb, and execute it from the command prompt.

Summary

In this chapter you learned that:

- When you download the setup file for Ruby under Windows, the setup file actually creates a simulation of the POSIX environment for Windows. Using the simulation environment, Ruby works under Windows.

- Rubywin is a complete IDE for Ruby on Windows. The Rubywin.exe file comes with the setup file.

- In Windows Explorer, each time you double-click a .rb file, the code in the file executes, and the command prompt window pops up and closes. However, when you double-click a .rbw file, the window does not open, and the code executes in the background.

- Using the Windows 32 API functions, you can access the low-level system features of the Windows operating system. Ruby provides the class WIN32API to access these functions.

- Ruby provides the Windows automation feature. Ruby acts like the Windows automation client, and the Windows automation server is Microsoft Word, Excel, or PowerPoint.

- To access the features of the automation server, Ruby provides a class WIN32OLE.

- All the methods unknown to the class WIN32OLE are handled by the method invoke of the class WIN32OLE.

- The method Range is used to insert values into the cells in Microsoft Excel.

- The method select is used to select a range of cells in Microsoft Excel.

- You specify a type to a chart by using the method Type.

- You insert text into a Word document by using the method Content of the Word document.

CHAPTER

12

Networking

Getting Started

The average person interacts with networks on a daily basis, be it through local-area networks (LANs) in our offices or the Internet. These networks provide indispensable links that reduce the time it takes us to communicate with each other. Ruby provides both general networking facilities and specialized classes that interact with Web and mail servers.

Perhaps the most fascinating networking facility is dRuby, which allows one program to interact directly with objects created by a program on another computer, anywhere in the world, as though the object resides in your own program!

In the following sections we will look at the basic facilities that are required for programs to interact across networks, including how to specify which other computers and applications we wish to communicate with, how to both initiate and accept connections, and how to use Ruby's higher-level classes to interact using standard Internet protocols such as the File Transfer Protocol (FTP), Hypertext Transfer Protocol (HTTP), and Post Office Protocol version 3 (POP3).

Basic Concepts

In most cases, there are two parties involved in any network communication. One is called the *client*, and the other is called the *server*. The browser you use to surf the World Wide Web is a client, whereas the pages you access are being provided to you by servers. Normally, a server accepts requests from many different clients. The clients initiate the connections, and the server accepts them.

To initiate a connection, a client needs to have some way to specify which program it wishes to communicate with. Because a single computer may run more than one server, for different purposes (e.g., a Web server and a mail server), we need to specify both the computer and the server with which we wish to make a connection.

The computer is specified by its *Internet Protocol (IP) address*. This is a set of four numbers, separated by periods. For example, 127.0.0.1 is an address that can be used to access programs on your own computer. Obviously, when we wish to access a computer on the other side of the world, determining the address we need could be difficult. Fortunately, in addition to IP addresses, networked computers normally are also given a mnemonic address consisting of a number of words separated by periods.

For example, www.ruby-lang.org is the name of the computer that runs the Web server containing Ruby's home page. The process by which a name such as this is translated into the corresponding IP address is beyond the scope of this book and normally happens transparently, so we really do not need to discuss it here. We almost always can use the mnemonic and ignore the numeric address.

Each server that runs on a computer accepts connections on a specific port number. For example, most Web servers accept connections on port number 80. When a server starts up, it indicates which IP address and port number it requires clients to use to access it. It then loops, accepting client requests and providing its services to them. Any client specifying the same IP address and port number will cause a connection to be made at the server.

> **NOTE** Some of the codes in this chapter might not work if your computer is connected to the Internet through a firewall. Your computer should have an external IP address.

TCP versus UDP

In the preceding section we mentioned that a server accepts client requests on a specific address and port number. There are two kinds of ports, Transmission Control Protocol (TCP) and User Datagram Protocol (UDP). For services that require medium to large amounts of data to be transferred, we use the protocol known as TCP. Such requests are called *connection-based*. For example, Web and mail servers use TCP. By contrast, the services provided by some programs require so little information to be transferred that a persistent connection is not necessary. Such programs use UDP port numbers. An example of this is a time server, where a single, very small piece of information is sent in response to any request. This is called *connectionless* access because no persistent connection is set up.

Obviously, both clients and servers need to specify whether they are using TCP or UDP. Because most services are provided via TCP, we will not discuss the details of UDP in this book.

Sockets

When we open a file, we are given a file handle, which differentiates one file from another, so that we can work with more than one file at a time. Similarly, when we create a connection between a client and a server, both ends of the connection are given a handle, called a *socket*. When the client writes data onto its socket, it appears, ready for reading, at the socket on the server, and vice versa.

Note that sockets are always bidirectional. In other words, they provide the same type of interface as a file opened in read/write using a mode of r+.

The Class TCPSocket

When a client wishes to connect to a server, the client constructs an instance of the class TCPSocket. For example, to connect to Ruby's Web server, we could use the following code:

```
require 'socket'
socket = TCPSocket.new("www.ruby-lang.org", 80)
socket.puts "GET /en/index.html"
while (line = socket.gets)
    puts line
end
socket.close
```

The statement require 'socket' gives the definition of the class TCPSocket. We then construct an instance, passing the name of the host running the Web server and the standard HTTP port number, namely, 80.

Once the TCPSocket object has been created, it works the same as any other IO object. We write our request to get the English-language Ruby home page /en/index.html and then read any lines that are returned.

The Class TCPServer

A simple server, wishing to accept connections, constructs an instance of the class TCPServer. Normally, you should not hard-code the IP address because it may change over time. There are two ways you can avoid doing so. You can either use a mnemonic address such as www.ruby-lang.org or simply specify a numeric address such as 0.0.0.0. The latter represents any address by which the local machine can be accessed.

To create a simple Web server, you can accept connections on the IP address 0.0.0.0 and the port number 80, as in the following code:

```
require 'socket'
server = TCPServer.new("0.0.0.0", 80)
loop do
# Wait for a connection from a client
  socket = server.accept
# Read the client's request
while socket.gets.chop.length > 0
# There's nothing to do here, because
# we don't care what the specific
```

```
# request is; we'll always send the
# same response.
end
# Write a header that says we can handle the
# request
socket.puts "HTTP/1.1 200 OK"
# Tell the client we're going to respond with
# HTML data
socket.puts "Content-type: text/html"
socket.puts ""
# Write a simple web page
socket.puts "<html>"
socket.puts "<body>"
socket.puts "<center>"
socket.puts "<h1>#{Time.now}</h1>"
socket.puts "</center>"
socket.puts "</body>"
socket.puts "</html>"
# Close the connection
socket.close
end
```

Figure 12.1 shows the output of this code.

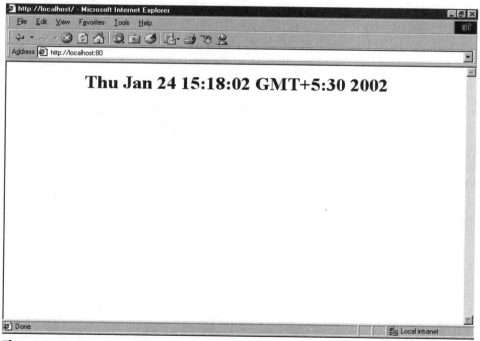

Figure 12.1   Browser output.

This code is relatively lengthy, but most of it is related to the fact that we are sending Hypertext Markup Language (HTML). As with the client, the most important thing is that we construct an instance of a networking class `TCPServer`. We then loop, accepting requests using `TCPServer.accept`. Each time the loop is executed, this will return a new `TCPSocket` instance connected to a client. We process the request and then close the socket.

The rest of the code is what is required to handle an HTTP request. First, we read everything up to a blank line, which tells us we have reached the end of the headers. We then send some headers to specify that we are able to handle the request (the `"HTTP/1.1 200 OK"`) and that the data we are sending the client are formatted as HTML (the `"Content-type: text/html"`).

Next we send our simple piece of HTML containing the current time as generated by constructing an instance of class `Time`, returned by `Time.now`. Finally, we close the socket and loop back to accept the next connection.

Accessing the Network

In the preceding section, you learned about the basics of networking. You also learned about the `TCPSocket` and `TCPServer` classes. In this section, you will go one step further and learn about how to access objects distributed in the network. You will also learn to write scripts to access Web pages, transfer files, or send and receive mails.

Distributed Ruby

One of the most interesting networking facilities that Ruby provides is the ability for one program to directly access an object residing inside another program, executing its methods as though the object were part of the client. This is similar to Java's Remote Method Invocation (RMI) but a lot easier to work with.

Here is a simple example of a server that provides access to a single object, in this case a simple counter that provides methods for incrementing its value and for obtaining its current value:

```
require 'drb'
class Counter
attr_reader:count
  def initialize
    @count = 0
```

```
    end
  def increment
    @count += 1
  end
end
counter = Counter.new
DRb.start_service("druby://localhost:8888", counter)
DRb.thread.join
```

First, we require the `drb` library. The class `Counter` itself is just like any other class. We have done nothing special to make it work across the network.

The command:

```
DRb.start_service("druby://localhost:8888", counter)
```

makes the `Counter` instance `counter` available for access by other programs. It gives the instance a Uniform Resource Locator (URL) beginning with `druby://`, just as a Web page has a URL beginning with `http://`. We specify a port number on which the access will take place. The second parameter to the `DRb.start_service` call is the object itself. Finally, we join the thread that `DRb.start_service` created so that the server will not exit.

Here is a simple client program that accesses the `Counter` object that has been exported by the server:

```
require 'drb'
DRb.start_service
counter = DRbObject.new(nil, "druby://localhost:8888")
5.times do
  counter.increment
  puts counter.count
end
```

Figure 12.2 shows the output of this code.

```
1
2
3
4
5
```

Figure 12.2 Output at the client end.

Again, we require drb to gain access to Distributed Ruby's facilities. We again call DRb.start_service, but this time we do not specify an object because we are not providing a service.

We gain access to the server's Counter object by constructing an instance of DRbObject, passing the same URL the server used to export the object.

The DRbObject instance is a wrapper that organizes for any calls we make to the methods of Counter to be shipped across the network to the actual object in the server. That object will execute the requested method, and the result will be shipped back to the client. To the client, it appears that the object is local.

Obviously, if we have many objects we wish to export across the network, rather than having a separate DRbObject instance for each one, it makes more sense to create a single object containing them all. For example, if we had multiple counters, we might do something like this:

```ruby
require 'drb'
class Counter
attr_reader :count
  def initialize
    @count = 0
  end
  def increment
    @count += 1
  end
end
class TrackedCounter < Counter
attr_reader :name
attr_reader :createdAt
attr_reader :lastAccess
  def initialize(name)
    super()
    @name = name
    @createdAt = Time.now
    @lastAccess = @createdAt
  end
end
tracked = TrackedCounter.new("Tracked Counter")
DRb.start_service("druby://localhost:8888", tracked)
DRb.thread.join
```

In this example we have created a slightly more complex class, TrackedCounter, that extends Counter by giving it a name and adding timestamps that track when the object was created and when it was last accessed.

Here is a simple client program that accesses the tracked object that has been exported by the server:

```
require 'drb'
DRb.start_service
tracked = DRbObject.new(nil, "druby://localhost:8888")
5.times do
  tracked.increment
  puts "The count is #{tracked.count}"
  puts "The last access date is #{tracked.lastAccess}"
end
```

Figure 12.3 shows the output of this code.

Now let's look at a common error. Imagine that instead of deriving a new class from Counter we had simply included a counter in Tracked-Counter. This sounds like quite a reasonable approach. However, if we try to do so, we will find that it ends up being a little messy. The reason is that we will need to provide proxy methods for each of the methods of Counter.

Why do we need to write proxies? Why can't the client program just call the methods of the encapsulated Counter instance? The answer is that we want to always see the current value of the counter, not its value as it was when we first obtained access to the TrackedCounter instance.

```
The count is 1
The last access date is Thu Jan 24 15:26:28 GMT+5:30 2002
The count is 2
The last access date is Thu Jan 24 15:26:28 GMT+5:30 2002
The count is 3
The last access date is Thu Jan 24 15:26:28 GMT+5:30 2002
The count is 4
The last access date is Thu Jan 24 15:26:28 GMT+5:30 2002
The count is 5
The last access date is Thu Jan 24 15:26:28 GMT+5:30 2002
```

Figure 12.3   Output at the client end.

Here is an (incorrect) implementation of `TrackedCounter` using composition rather than inheritance:

```ruby
require 'drb'
class Counter
attr_reader:count
  def initialize
    @count = 0
  end
  def increment
    @count += 1
  end
end
class TrackedCounter
attr_accessor:ourCounter
attr_reader:name
attr_reader:createdAt
attr_reader:lastAccess
  def initialize(name)
    @ourCounter = Counter.new
    @name = name
    @createdAt = Time.now
    @lastAccess = @createdAt
  end
end
bad = TrackedCounter.new("Bad Counter")
DRb.start_service("druby://localhost:8888", bad)
DRb.thread.join
```

As you can see, this class contains an instance of `Counter`, called `ourCounter`, and we have provided an accessor so that the client code can see it.

Now consider this piece of client code using our composite server class:

```ruby
require 'drb'
  DRb.start_service
  bad = DRbObject.new(nil, "druby://localhost:8888")
  puts "#{bad.name} was created at #{bad.createdAt}"
  puts "Before: last access is #{bad.lastAccess}"
  puts "#{bad.name} = #{bad.ourCounter.count}"
```

The important thing is that the calls to `bad.createdAt` and `bad.lastAccess` work because they are methods of the class `Tracked-Counter`, and we have a distributed instance of that class. However, the call to `bad.ourCounter.count` fails because `bad.ourCounter` is a normal object, not a distributed object. Hence, trying to call one of its methods remotely will fail. Thus you get the error as shown in Figure 12.4.

```
Bad Counter was created at Thu Jan 17 16:56:21 GMT+5:30 2002
Before: last access is Thu Jan 17 16:56:21 GMT+5:30 2002
client.rb:6: undefined method `count' for #<DRb::DRbUnknown:0x4587860> (NameErro
r)
```

Figure 12.4   Error in the code.

Even if the object returned by our counter actually was a `Counter`, we would still have a problem. This instance would be local to our client program. Thus, if the remote `Counter` subsequently were incremented, we would not see the new value. Similarly, if we were to increment our counter, the remote one would not be updated.

Effectively, what we are seeing here is that `dRuby` provides only a shallow interface to the objects we export. If we want to give the client access to anything lower down, we need to provide methods that do that access on the server side and pass back the results.

For the reasons discussed here, if we wish to export a container of objects such as an array or hash using `dRuby`, we need to provide accessors to get at the contents of those containers.

Accessing Web Pages Using Net::HTTP

We normally use a browser to view the pages provided by servers on the World Wide Web. However, it sometimes might be handy if we could access the contents of pages using a script. For example, many news sites are updated on a daily basis. We can pull down the contents from a number of such sites each morning and summarize them or translate them into another format that is more useful to us. For instance, we might like to transfer the information into our personal organizer to read on the way to work.

We saw earlier in this chapter how we could write a small client using `TCPSocket` to access the contents of a page. This is such a common task that the standard Ruby library provides a class `Net::HTTP` that encapsulates the details to save us coding it ourselves.

Here is an equivalent to our preceding example, this time using `Net::HTTP`:

```
require 'net/http'
# Connect to the server on port 80 ...
home = Net::HTTP.new("www.ruby-lang.org", 80)
# Retrieve the text of the main page (response will
# contain "OK" if our access was successful) ...
```

```
response, text = home.get("/en/index.html", nil)
# Display the page's content ...
puts text
```

This is obviously much simpler than the code we wrote ourselves! Note that we provide basically the same information we did previously: the mnemonic address of the server, www.ruby-lang.org; the port number, 80; and the specific page we wish to download, /en/index.html.

Moving Files Around Using Net::FTP

The class Net::FTP provides access to the FTP used to move files between computers. It can be used to both download and upload files. Here is a simple program that downloads the latest stable snapshot of Ruby from the Ruby server:

```
require 'net/ftp'
# Connect to the FTP server on the Ruby home site ...
ftp = Net::FTP.new("ftp.ruby-lang.org")
# Log in anonymously ...
ftp.login
# Use passive mode, in case we're behind a firewall
# that requires it ...
ftp.passive = true
# Change to the right directory ...
files = ftp.chdir("/pub/ruby")
# Download the latest Ruby snapshot (storing it locally,
# using the same name) ...
snapshot = "stable-snapshot.tar.gz"
ftp.getbinaryfile(snapshot, snapshot)
#Finally, close the connection to the FTP server
ftp.close
```

We gain access to the server by constructing an instance of Net::FTP. We then log in to the server; in this case, we do not specify a name or password (that is, we are logging in anonymously).

Why we set the instance variable passive to true is beyond the scope of our discussion. This is often necessary if we are behind a firewall, which is the case for most users. Setting it should not cause any problems if we are not behind a firewall, so we simply do it every time.

The snapshot is always found in a particular directory on the FTP server, so we move there. We do not really need to do this; we could instead specify the full path for the file as part of the next step. However, by doing this, if something goes wrong, we will be able to tell more easily whether it was because we got the directory wrong or because the file was not there (because our program would abort on a different line in these two cases).

Finally, we download the file. We use binary mode because it is a compressed Tape Archive (TAR) file, and then we close the connection.

Sending Mail Using Net::SMTP

To send email messages, you generally talk to a Simple Mail Transfer Protocol (SMTP) server. Ruby provides the class Net::SMTP for this purpose. Suppose that you want to send email to Fred Bloggs, whose email address is fred@bloggs.com. Here is the code:

```
# Gain access to a mail server
require "net/smtp"
LIBRARIAN = "librarian@knowledge.inc.com"
smtp = Net::SMTP.new(MAIL_SERVER)
smtp.start()
# Specify the recipient of this message
address = "fred@bloggs.com"
# Send the e-mail
smtp.ready(LIBRARIAN, address) do |mail|
mail.write "Subject: A small test\r\n"
mail.write "\r\n"
mail.write "Hi Fred,\r\n"
mail.write "\r\n"
mail.write "We hope you are making the most\r\n"
mail.write "of the library's facilities.\r\n"
mail.write "\r\n"
mail.write "If you would like any assistance,\r\n"
mail.write "please do not hesitate to contact\r\n"
mail.write "us at any time.\r\n"
mail.write "\r\n"
mail.write "Yours sincerely,\r\n"
mail.write "\r\n"
mail.write "Our Friendly Library Staff\r\n"
end
```

NOTE While creating the instance of Net::SMTP, replace MAIL_SERVER with the address of your mail server.

First, we define which mail server we would like to use to send the message by constructing an instance of Net::SMTP specifying the address of the server. Then we connect to the mail server by using Net::SMTP#start. If the mail server requires authentication, we pass our login and password at this stage.

Finally, we call Library#ready, passing it the email address of the recipient, and then we write the mail message to the IO instance that is connected to the server. We need to be careful to leave a blank line after all the headers. In this case we have only one header, the subject. Once the block of code passed to `Library#ready` completes, the email will have been accepted by the server and hopefully will be on its way to the intended recipient.

Reading Mail Using Net::POP3

Ruby provides the class `Net::POP3` class for access to mail servers via POP3, which is the de facto standard on the Internet. Here is a simple program that reads the first message currently in a mailbox:

```
require "net/pop"
# Connect to the POP3 server
pop = Net::POP3.new("pop3.zipworld.com.au")
# Initiate a session, by logging in to the
# mail server
pop.start("harryo", "secret") do |pop|
  # Read the first message
  msg = pop.mails[0]
  # Print the 'From:' header line
  puts msg.header.split("\r\n").grep(/^From: /)
  # Write the message to $stdout
  puts "\nFull message:\n"
  msg.all($stdout)
end
```

And here is the output we received in a run of this program after sending a simple test message to one mail server:

```
From: Harry Ohlsen <harryo@zip.com.au>
Full message:
Received: by mangalore (mbox harryo)
(with Cubic Circle's cucipop (v1.31 1998/05/13) Thu Dec 27 12:40:37
2001)
X-From_: harryo@zip.com.au Thu Dec 27 12:40:03 2001
Return-Path: <harryo@zip.com.au>
Message-Id: <200112270140.MAA02340@mangalore.zipworld.com.au>
Received: from there ([144.135.24.78]) by mta02bw.bigpond.com
(Netscape Messaging Server 4.15) with SMTP id GOZBM900.21J for
<harryo@zip.com.au>; Thu, 27 Dec 2001 11:46:57 +1000
Content-Type: text/plain;
charset="iso-8859-15"
From: Harry Ohlsen <harryo@zip.com.au>
Reply-To: harryo@zip.com.au
To: harryo@zip.com.au
Subject: Testing, testing, testing!
Date: Thu, 27 Dec 2001 12:40:24 +1100
X-Mailer: KMail [version 1.3.1]
```

```
MIME-Version: 1.0
Content-Transfer-Encoding: 8bit
This is a quick demonstration message.
```

Now we will use the scenario of Knowledge Inc., to send automatic email messages.

Sending Automatic Emails

Problem Statement

To provide better service to its customers, Knowledge Inc., would like to send an automatic email message to any customer who has books due back in the near future. We can run a script each night that finds any users to whom we should send an email and use the class `Net::SMTP` to send it.

Task List

- ✔ **Write code to find all appropriate customers.**
- ✔ **Generate an email message for all identified customers.**
- ✔ **Send the message to the customers.**
- ✔ **Save and execute the code.**
- ✔ **Verify the output.**

Write Code to Find All Appropriate Customers

First, we need to create a few simple classes to represent customers, their loans, and the respective books:

```
class Book
attr_reader :title
  def initialize(title)
    @title = title
  end
end
class Loan
attr_reader :book
attr_reader :dueDate
  def initialize(book, loanPeriod)
    @book = book
    @dueDate = Time.now + (loanPeriod * DAYS)
  end
end
```

```
class Customer
attr_reader :name
attr_reader :emailAddress
attr_reader :loans
  def initialize(name, emailAddress)
    @name = name
    @emailAddress = emailAddress
    @loans  = []
  end
  def add_loan(book, dueDate)
    loan = Loan.new(book, dueDate)
    @loans.push(loan)
  end
end
```

We see that a book is simply represented by its title, a loan contains a reference to the book that has been borrowed plus the date it is due back, and a customer has a name, an email address, and a list of his or her currently outstanding loans. The method `Customer#add_loan` adds a book to the list of loans for that customer.

Now we need to create the class `Library` that tracks all the library's customers and what loans they have:

```
DAYS = 24 * 60 * 60 # Number of seconds in a day
SOON = 4# Definition of "soon", in days
MAIL_SERVER = "mail-hub"  # The mail server
class Library
attr_accessor :customers
  def initialize
    @customers = []
  end
  def add_customer(customer)
    @customers.push(customer)
  end
  def send_reminders
    today = Time.now
# For each customer ...
    @customers.each do |customer|
# Create an array of loans that are due soon ...
      dueSoon = []
# For each loan ...
      customer.loans.each do |loan|
# See how many days there are until it
# is due to be returned ...
        days = loan.dueDate - today
# If the due date is close, add it to
# the list ...
        if days <= (SOON * DAYS)
```

```
        dueSoon.push(loan)
      end
    end
# If this customer has any loans due soon, send
# them an e-mail, detailing which books they are
# and when they are due ...
    if dueSoon.length > 0
mail_reminders(customer, dueSoon)
    end
      end
      end
end
```

`Library#add_customer` adds a new person to the library's list of customers. `Library#send_reminders` finds all the customers who have books on loan that are due soon, creating an array of loans that are due for return soon. If a given customer has any outstanding loans that are due sometime soon, `Library#send_reminders` calls `Library#mail_reminder` to send the email.

Generate an Email Message for All Identified Customers

We need to run through the list of loans that are due soon and create an appropriate message:

```
MAIL_SERVER = "mail-hub"
def create_email(customer, dueSoon)
message = ""
message << "Subject: Loans due back within #{SOON} days\r\n"
message << "\r\n"
message << "Dear #{customer.name},\r\n"
message << "\r\n"
message << "The following books are due back soon:\r\n"
message << "\r\n"
dueSoon.each do |loan|
message << "  #{loan.dueDate.to_s[0, 10]}" <<
           " #{loan.book.title}"
end
message
end
```

The most important thing here is that we have a header prefixed by `Subject:`, followed by a blank line, which signifies the end of the headers. We need to define `MAIL_SERVER` to be the network address of the computer that contains the SMTP server.

Send the Message to the Customer

Now we come to the most important part of this case study. How do we send the email? Here is the code for `Library#mail_reminders`:

```
LIBRARIAN = "librarian@knowledge.inc.com"
def mail_reminders(customer, dueSoon)
# Create the mail message ...
message = create_email(customer, dueSoon)
# Gain access to a mail server ...
smtp = Net::SMTP.new(MAIL_SERVER)
smtp.start()
# Specify the recipient of this message ...
address = customer.emailAddress
# Send the e-mail ...
smtp.ready(LIBRARIAN, address) do |mail|
mail << message
end
end
```

Finally, here is a code that uses the classes we have written to actually send the email:

```
# Create the library department
library = Library.new
# Create a few customers
anthony = Customer.new("Anthony", "anthony@isp.com")
tom = Customer.new("Tom", "tom@isp.com")
harry = Customer.new("Harry", "harry@isp.com")
jerry = Customer.new("Jerry", "jerry@isp.com")
# Create a few books ...
warAndPeace = Book.new("War and Peace")
prideAndPrejudice = Book.new("Pride and Prejudice")
mobyDick = Book.new("Moby Dick")
frankenstein = Book.new("Frankenstein")
dracula = Book.new("Dracula")
snowWhite = Book.new("Snow White")
# Loan the customers some books
anthony.add_loan(warAndPeace, 3)
anthony.add_loan(mobyDick, 4)
tom.add_loan(dracula, 2)
harry.add_loan(snowWhite, 3)
jerry.add_loan(prideAndPrejudice, 5)
jerry.add_loan(frankenstein, 7)
# Make them customers of the library
library.add_customer(anthony)
library.add_customer(tom)
library.add_customer(harry)
library.add_customer(jerry)
# Ask the library to send out the reminders
library.send_reminders
```

Save and Execute the Code

Save all the code we have seen in the preceding sections as `reminders.rb`, and execute it from the command prompt by typing `ruby reminders.rb`.

You obviously will need to find out what your actual mail server's name is and replace the email addresses of our fake customers with some real addresses.

Verify the Output

Check that email messages are sent to the appropriate customers, in other words, those who had loans that were due back in four days or less: Anthony, Tom, and Harry. Check also that the email messages refer to the correct loans.

Summary

In this chapter you learned that:

- Network communication takes place between a client and server.
- TCP is a connection-based protocol.
- TCP is used when medium to large amounts of data need to be transferred.
- UDP is a connectionless-based protocol.
- UDP is used when small amounts of data need to be transferred.
- A socket is used to create a connection between a client and a server. In a network connection, a socket is present at both the client end and the server end. The client talks to the server by using the client socket, whereas the server responds by using the server socket.
- Creating an instance of the class `TCPSocket` creates a client socket, whereas creating an instance of the class `TCPServer` creates a server socket.
- Using distributed Ruby, you can access from one program an object of another program and execute the methods of the object. Distributed Ruby is similar to Java's RMI.
- Using the class `Net::HTTP`, you can invoke the HTTP and therefore can access Web pages.
- Using the class `Net::FTP`, you can invoke the FTP and therefore can move files from one computer to another.

- Using the class Net::SMTP, you can talk to a mail server and therefore can send email.
- To send email, the SMTP is used.
- Using the class Net::POP3, you can talk to a mail server and therefore can read email.
- To read email, the POP3 is used.

Ruby Extensions

There are several existing libraries in different languages that provide functionality that is useful for programs. It would not be logical for us to rewrite all these libraries in Ruby when we can use them readily. Moreover, at times, we may need better performance than can be obtained from an interpreted language such as Ruby. In such a situation, it would be useful to write or use the time-critical code in a more efficient language and simply call it from our Ruby code.

Fortunately, Ruby provides facilities that allow us to handle both these situations. We can quite easily write extensions in C that hook seamlessly into the environment of Ruby. They can be made to look to our programs as though they are other pieces of Ruby code. We can even go the other way and embed a complete Ruby interpreter into a C program. This would allow us to use its scripting facilities instead of having to write our own purpose-built engine.

Ruby with C

To give us something to talk about, here is a trivial example that implements a class called Simple with two instance variables, a Fixnum called @i and an Array called @a:

```c
#include "ruby.h"
/*
 *  Definition of Simple_initialize ...
 */
static VALUE simple_initialize(VALUE self, int iValue)
{
    rb_iv_set(self, "@i", iValue);
    rb_iv_set(self, "@a", rb_ary_new());
    return self;
}
/*
 *  Define accessors for @i and @a ...
 */
static VALUE simple_get_i(VALUE self)
{
    return rb_iv_get(self, "@i");
}
static VALUE simple_set_i(VALUE self, int iValue)
{
    return rb_iv_set(self, "@i", iValue);
}
static VALUE simple_get_a(VALUE self)
{
    return rb_iv_get(self, "@a");
}
/*
** The code that constructs the Simple class itself ...
*/
void Init_Simple()
{
    /*
     *  A variable to store the Simple class we are about
     *  to create ...
     */
    VALUE cSimple;
    /*
     *  Ask the Ruby interpreter to create a class
     *  called Simple ...
     */
    cSimple = rb_define_class("Simple", rb_cObject);
    /*
     *  Tell it what function to call to initialize
     *  an instance of Simple ...
     */
```

```
      */
      rb_define_method(cSimple, "initialize",
                       simple_initialize, 1);
      /*
       * Define get and set accessors for @i and a get
       * accessor for @a ...
       */
      rb_define_method(cSimple, "i",  simple_get_i, 0);
      rb_define_method(cSimple, "i=", simple_set_i, 1);
      rb_define_method(cSimple, "a",  simple_get_a, 0);
  }
```

In this example we have included the header file ruby.h. This defines all the C datatypes and functions that allow us to interact with the Ruby interpreter.

The next thing that is prominent is the general use of the keyword VALUE. This is a hold-all type that is used to store data in a form that can be deciphered by the Ruby interpreter. Various functions are available to convert between VALUE and all the standard C datatypes such as int and double. There are also functions that create standard Ruby datatypes such as Array and Hash.

Now let's take a look at the Init_Simple function at the bottom of the code. The interpreter calls this function when it encounters the require 'Simple' statement in our Ruby source code. The purpose of the require 'Simple' statement is to create the class Simple. This involves defining the new class and adding four methods: the initializer and three accessor functions for the instance variables @i and @a.

We can see that rb_define_class() accepts two parameters. The first is the name of the class we are creating. The second argument rb_cObject is a reference to the standard Ruby class Object that will be the parent for our new class. If we wanted the class Simple to have a different parent, we would specify that class here. We store the value returned by rb_define_class() in our own variable called cSimple, which is our reference to the newly created class. We need to pass that reference to any functions that access our new class.

Next, we inform the interpreter to associate certain C functions with the methods of the class Simple. First, we define Simple.initialize. We pass in cSimple to inform rb_define_method() about the class to which we want to add the method. We then pass the name of the method, which is initialize in this case. Then we pass the name of the function we wish it to call when that method is referenced in our Ruby code (in this case, simple_initialize()) and finally a number that specifies how many arguments the method accepts (in this case, 1).

This causes the interpreter to organize in such a way that whenever `Simple.initialize` is called, our C function `simple_initialize()` will be called.

Let's look at the code for `simple_initialize()`. Note that we said that this function is passed one argument, but the code actually accepts two! An instance method of a class will be called for many different objects. Therefore, we need to know to which object each call refers.

This implies that, as its name suggests, the first parameter is the equivalent of `self` for the object we are initializing. Therefore, we do not need to include it while calculating the number of actual parameters to the method. We instead refer only to the number of parameters that will be passed to `Simple.initialize` in the Ruby code.

Each line of `simple_initialize()` uses the function `rb_iv_set()` to create an instance variable (this is what `iv` refers to) for the object we are initializing.

In the case of `@i`, we simply pass the integer value that was provided. For `@a`, however, we need to create a C representation of a Ruby `Array`. We do this by calling `rb_ary_new()`.

Now let's look at the other lines of `Init_Simple`. They associate three more functions with the corresponding methods of our new class. The first two define `get` and `set` accessors for `@i`, and the last one defines a `get` accessor for `@a`.

Compiling a New Class

Before we can use our new class, we need to compile the C code and organize it in such a way that the Ruby interpreter can access it. Assuming the absence of any syntax errors, this is quite easy. In Ruby, you can create a `Makefile` for any specific environment. All we need to do is write a short Ruby file and run it. Here is the file for our new class, which is conventionally called `extconf.rb`:

```
require 'mkmf'
create_makefile("Simple")
```

Most of the real work happens inside `mkmf`, which contains the method `create_makefile`. We pass this method the name of our class, and it does the rest. After we run this code through the interpreter by typing `ruby` **extconf.rb,** we will find a new file called `Makefile` in our directory. This file contains carefully crafted compilation statements, which we will not discuss here.

Note that `Makefile` expects the C source code for our class to be stored in a file whose name is the same as that of the class. However, this name is specified in lowercase letters with an extension of .c. For example, for the class `Simple`, the name of the file should be `simple.c`.

To compile the new class, type `make`. Assuming everything compiles correctly, you should end up with a file called either `Simple.so` or `Simple.dll` depending on whether you are running UNIX or Windows. This is a dynamic library containing the compiled C code.

To make this new class accessible universally instead of only when you are in the current directory, you need to execute the `make install` command. This will copy the library to the correct place for our installation.

Using Our New Class

After we have built our library, we can use the class `Simple` as though it had been written directly in Ruby:

```
require 'Simple'
# Construct an object of class Simple, with @i initialised
# to 123 ...
s = Simple.new(123)
# Print the values of @i and @a.  This calls
# simple_get_i() and simple_get_a() ...
puts s.i          # => 123
puts s.a.inspect # => []
# Change the value of @i. This calls simple_set_i() ...
s.i = 456
puts s.i # => 456
# Append a couple of strings to @a ...
s.a.push("Hello")
s.a.push("World!")
puts s.a.inspect # => ["Hello", "World!"]
```

When the interpreter encounters `require 'Simple'`, it loads the dynamic library recently created and calls `Init_Simple()`, which creates the global object that represents this class. When asked to construct a new instance of the class `Simple` by using the statement `Simple.new`, the new object is allocated memory, and the argument of the new method is passed to `simple_initialize()`. When the code reads the values of @i or @a, the appropriate `get` function is called. When we ask for @i to be assigned the new value `456`, the interpreter calls `simple_set_i()`. Therefore, we now have our own C code that implements a new class.

Interfacing to Existing Libraries

There might be situations where you would like to access an existing C library. We now have all the tools we need to do this. For example, the standard Ruby module Math provides access to the sin() and cos() functions from the standard maths library but not to their inverse functions asin() and acos().

We write the following module called MoreMath with a few functions to gain access to them:

```
#include "ruby.h"
#include "math.h"
/*
 * Define module functions to access asin() and acos() ...
 */
static VALUE moremath_acos(VALUE module, VALUE x)
{
    return rb_float_new(acos(NUM2DBL(x)));
}
static VALUE moremath_asin(VALUE module, VALUE x)
{
    return rb_float_new(asin(NUM2DBL(x)));
}
/*
** The code that constructs the MoreMath module ...
*/
void Init_MoreMath()
{
    /*
     * A variable to store the MoreMath module we are about
     * to create ...
     */
    VALUE mMoreMath;
    /*
     * Ask the Ruby interpreter to create a module
     * called MoreMath ...
     */
    mMoreMath = rb_define_module("MoreMath");
    /*
     * Define module functions to access acos() and asin() ...
     */
    rb_define_module_function(mMoreMath, "acos", moremath_acos, 1);
    rb_define_module_function(mMoreMath, "asin", moremath_asin, 1);
}
```

In this case, we have defined a new module called MoreMath instead of a class. We have defined two module functions that simply pass on our request to the standard library routines and return the results to the interpreter, converting them to the Ruby Float datatype first.

Note the calls to NUM2DBL() and rb_float_new() in the two functions we are exporting to the Ruby interpreter. The former converts a VALUE into a normal C double. The latter uses a double to create a new Ruby Float object.

Here is an example that uses MoreMath. It should be fairly straightforward if you remember a bit of basic trigonometry.

```
require 'MoreMath'
# The cosine of PI is -1, so if we take acos(-1), we
# should get PI ...
puts "PI = #{MoreMath.acos(-1)}" # => 3.141592654
# Similarly, the sine of PI/2 is 1, so taking asin(1)
# and multiplying by 2 should also give us PI ...
puts "PI = #{2 * MoreMath.asin(1)}" # => 3.141592654
# Let's just print what Math thinks PI is, to see whether
# these values look correct ...
puts "Math::PI = #{Math::PI}" # => 3.141592654
```

Embedding a Ruby Interpreter into a C Program

We mentioned earlier about the facility to embed a copy of the Ruby interpreter in a C program. Imagine that we are building an image-manipulation tool. It might be nice to allow users to script some of their complex tasks, permitting them to perform a complex set of manipulations on hundreds of images without any user interaction later being required.

One approach to create our image-manipulation tool would be to create our own customized language in which the user can define the required manipulations. However, as specified in relation to third-party libraries, why do you need to reinvent the wheel when we have a useful scripting engine — Ruby!

The interpreter has been designed carefully so that it also can be embedded in an arbitrary C program. All we need to do is link it in with our program, call a couple of functions to initialize it, and then we can begin using Ruby for scripting.

Consider the following example:

```
int main(int argc, char *argv[])
{
    /*
     *  Initialise the image manipulation engine ...
     */
    init_graphics_engine();
    /*
     *  Initialise the Ruby interpreter ...
     */
```

```
        ruby_init();
        /*
         *  Define the name of the script ...
         */
        ruby_script("graphics");
        /*
         *  Load the user's set of manipulations, in
         *  the form of a Ruby script ...
         */
        rb_load_file("manipulations.rb");
        /*
         *  Execute their script ...
         */
        ruby_run();
    }
```

The comments in this code snippet explain pretty much everything you need to know. We will assume that calling `init_graphics_engine()` performs any startup that is required for our graphics tool. We then initialize the Ruby interpreter, name the script, load the set of manipulations the user wants to run in the form of a Ruby script from a file called `manipulations.rb`, and then ask the embedded Ruby interpreter to execute the script.

Image processing is a CPU-intensive task. Therefore, it is possible that we create a few C extensions to perform various kinds of manipulations by using the techniques described earlier. The script would then be written in relation to the classes and/or modules those extensions provide.

Two existing examples of using an embedded Ruby interpreter are eRuby and modRuby. Both allow the user to embed Ruby code into HTML files similar to Cold Fusion, Active Server Pages (ASP) or Hypertext Pre-Processor (PHP), providing dynamic content creation. Both take slightly different approaches to the problem. eRuby is a program that accepts as its input HTML containing embedded Ruby code. eRuby executes the embedded Ruby code to generate pure HTML, which is then passed back to the client's browser. Alternatively, modRuby is a library module that hooks into and becomes part of the Apache Web server.

Obtaining More Information

This short discussion has only scratched the surface of what is possible. You will find a lot of the details in the file README.EXT that comes with the source-code distribution of Ruby, which is something you will need before you begin working with extensions.

Safety Issues

When we write and run programs, we can use the code to perform numerous actions. However, it is important to protect these programs from inexperienced or malicious users, especially if these are accessible on the Internet or even the local network.

Ruby is a very powerful language with features that allow dynamic execution of code that is created while the program runs. For example, `eval` can be used to run a piece of Ruby code that does not even exist in the source of our program. Consider the following example:

```ruby
loop do
    $stderr.print "Enter An Expression: "
    if (command = gets)
        begin
            puts "   #{eval command}"
        rescue
            puts "That doesn't seem to be a valid expression."
        end
    else
        break
    end
end
```

Each time the user enters a string, we use `eval` to execute it and then output the result. For example, if the user entered 2 + 2, the output would be 4. This makes for a nice little calculator. If the user enters an invalid expression, an exception will be raised so that the program does not abort.

We have used `$stderr` (normally unbuffered) because otherwise the prompt would not be displayed. Now consider what happens if the user enters `system('rm *')`. The program would evaluate that expression and remove all the files in the current directory as a consequence.

It is possible that this is not a problem if the user is running this program as a normal user. The reason is that the security mechanisms in the file system ensure that a normal user cannot delete the important system files. However, if this program were running as someone else, say, root, then we would be in serious trouble.

Ruby uses the concept of *tainting* of objects and safety levels to reduce these types of security risks.

Tainting

Ruby automatically marks any data that comes from outside the program as tainted. This includes strings read from files or over a network connection and the values of environment variables. Anything we wrote directly in the source code of our program can be considered inherently kosher because if we did not want it that way, we would not have written it that way. However, any data that are tainted because they came from outside our source code should be viewed with suspicion.

Any other objects that have been created using tainted data are potentially problematic. Therefore, the interpreter also marks as tainted any object that is derived from a tainted object in some way.

The class `Object`, from which all other classes are derived, provides the method `tainted` that allows us to determine whether a given object is tainted. To see how tainting works, let's look at few examples:

```
# First, we'll just create a couple of variables directly
# within our program ...
hello = "Hello"
puts hello.tainted? # => false
helloWorld = hello + ", world!"
puts hello.tainted? # => false
# Now, let's look at something from our environment.  The
# following should work on a Unix machine ...
login = ENV["LOGNAME"]
puts login.tainted? # => true
myLogin = "My login name is #{login}"
```

```
puts myLogin.tainted? # => true
# Now, we know that our variable "hello" is currently
# untainted, # so let's try appending the tainted
# variable "login" ...
hello << ", my login is #{login}"
puts hello.tainted? # => true
# But, "helloWorld", which was originally derived from
# "hello" should not be affected, even though "hello"
# has become tainted ...
puts helloWorld.tainted? # => false
```

Levels of Safety

Why do you need to mark objects as tainted? We have seen that using `eval` on tainted object can cause problems. There are many other things for which they should not be used, such as the paths of directories to be removed and the names of programs to `exec`.

Instead of simply disallowing everything that potentially could be dangerous when applied to tainted data, Ruby provides the global variable `$SAFE` to allow the programmer to define the level of risk that is acceptable.

If `$SAFE` has a value of 0, which is normal unless the program is being run `setuid` or `setgid` root, there are no limitations on using tainted data. The higher the value of `$SAFE`, the more tightly does the interpreter constrain the use of tainted objects.

We may start out at the default safety level of 0, create a few objects to be used as the accepted environment in which our program will run, and then increase `$SAFE` to avoid the user modifying that environment.

Index